Music Express
Year 1

LESSON PLANS, RECORDINGS,
ACTIVITIES, PHOTOCOPIABLES
AND VIDEOCLIPS

Series devised by **Maureen Hanke**

Compiled by **Helen MacGregor**   Illustrated by **Alison Dexter**   Edited by **Sheena Roberts**

A & C Black • London

Contents

First published 2002
Reprinted 2002, 2003, 2004
A & C Black Publishers Ltd
37, Soho Square, London W1D 3QZ
© 2002 A & C Black Publishers Ltd

Teaching text © Helen MacGregor 2002
Unit headings, unit summary text, learning objectives and outcomes © Qualifications and Curriculum Authority
CD/Videoclips compilation © A & C Black 2002
Edited by Sheena Roberts
Designed by Jocelyn Lucas
Cover illustration © Alex Ayliffe 2002
Inside illustrations © Alison Dexter 2002
Audio CD sound engineering by Stephen Chadwick
Videoclips filmed and edited by Jamie Acton-Bond
CD-ROM post production by Ian Shepherd
at Sound Recording Technology

Printed in Great Britain by Caligraving Ltd, Thetford, Norfolk

A & C Black uses paper produced with elemental chlorine-free pulp, harvested from managed sustainable forests.

A CIP catalogue record for this book is available from the British Library.

Introduction

About Music Express

Music Express provides teaching activities that are imaginative, inspiring and fun.

It has been written especially for classroom teachers. It is:

- user-friendly;
- well planned;
- fully resourced, and
- no music reading is required.

Using Music Express as a scheme of work

National Curriculum

Music Express fulfils the requirements of the Music National Curriculum of England, of Wales and of Northern Ireland and the 5-14 National Guidelines for Scotland.

Learning with *Music Express*, children will gain a broad and balanced musical education. They will:

- learn about and sing songs from around the world including the British Isles;
- learn about music from different periods and genres;
- enjoy music lessons with a balance of listening, composing, performing and appraising.

A steady progression plan has been built into *Music Express*, both within each book and from one year to the next, ensuring consistent musical development.

Opportunities are identified throughout for evaluating the children's work and monitoring their progress.

The English QCA scheme of work for music

Music Express is based on the structure of the QCA scheme of work. It uses the same unit headings, making it easy to navigate, and provides activities to achieve the learning outcomes stated.

The teaching activities in *Music Express* have been drawn from and inspired by A & C Black's extensive classroom music resources.

The units

There are six units in each book. Below is a list of the units in *Music Express Year 1*, as described by the QCA:

Sounds interesting
'This unit develops children's ability to identify different sounds and to change and use sounds expressively in response to a stimulus.'

The long and the short of it
'This unit develops children's ability to discriminate between longer and shorter sounds, and to use them to create interesting sequences of sound.'

Feel the pulse
'This unit develops children's ability to recognise the difference between pulse and rhythm and to perform with a sense of pulse.'

Taking off
'This unit develops children's ability to discriminate between higher and lower sounds and to create simple melodic patterns.'

What's the score?
'This unit develops children's ability to recognise different ways sounds are made and changed and to name, and know how to play, a variety of classroom instruments.'

Rain rain go away
'This unit develops children's ability to recognise how sounds and instruments can be used expressively and combined to create music in response to a stimulus.'

The lessons

Each unit is divided into six, weekly lessons, which are intended to be taught over a half term.

There are three activities per lesson which may be taught in one longer music lesson, or over three shorter lessons to suit your timetable.

Planning

The CD-ROM

The CD-ROM provides a medium term plan and six, weekly lesson plans for each unit. These may be printed out to go in your planning folder.

Whilst it is not necessary when teaching the activities to have the lesson plan alongside, it contains useful information for preparing your lesson. This includes:

- the learning objectives and outcomes;

- a list of the resources and minimal preparation you will need to do before the lesson;

- a vocabulary section which defines the musical terms appropriate to the lesson;

- a suggestion of ways to provide differentiated support for particular activities;

- a lesson extension - a suggestion for taking the lesson further with individuals or the whole class. (The extension activities are particularly useful when teaching a mixed year-group class as they extend the older and/or more able children.)

The book

The book provides step by step teaching notes for each lesson. These are written to be as easy to follow as possible.

There are photocopiables to supplement many of the activities.

Preparation

Music Express is designed to minimise your preparation time.

Look out for the icons next to the activity headings which indicate things you need to prepare.

Key to icons

 Photocopiable icon: some activities require photocopies or activity cards to be made from a particular photocopiable.

 Black CD icon: these tracks are for the children to listen to during an activity.

 Grey CD icon: these tracks are for your reference.

 Videoclip and picture icons: you will need to have access to a computer for an activity to show videoclips and pictures on the CD-ROM. (You might like to use a computer-compatible projector to show the videoclips and pictures on a screen for the whole class to see more easily.)

Other resources

Classroom percussion

You will need to have a range of classroom percussion instruments available.

Many activities suggest several members of the class playing instruments at the same time. If necessary, pupils could share instruments and take turns to play.

Specific activities recommend the instruments you will need, but you should use the instruments that you have available.

For a class of 30 pupils, aim to have at least the following:

- Tuned percussion
    - 1 alto xylophone
    - 1 alto metallophone
    - 1 set of chime bars
    - a selection of beaters
- A range of untuned percussion instruments, eg
    - tambours
    - drums
    - wood blocks
    - cabassas
    - maracas

- Other interesting soundmakers, eg

  ocean drum

  rainmaker

  whistles

  wind chimes

- Electronic keyboards are a very useful resource and should be included wherever possible.

Instrumental lessons

Wherever appropriate, invite members of the class who are having instrumental lessons to bring their instruments into classroom music lessons.

If you are not sure which notes particular instruments use, ask the child's instrumental teacher.

Recording and evaluating

Recording on cassette or video

Have a cassette recorder and blank audio cassettes available during your music lessons. Recording pupils' work is important for monitoring their progress.

Children enjoy listening to their performances and contributing to the evaluation of their own and their classmates' work.

Many activities include movement as well as music. If you have a video camera available, video the performance. If not, invite members of your class or another class to watch and offer feedback.

Help for teachers

Teaching tips and background information

These are provided throughout next to the activity or activities to which they refer.

Dance and movement

Encourage movement in activities where it is not mentioned - it is an important means of musical learning.

Group work

The activities suggest appropriate group sizes. Be flexible, especially if your class has little or no experience of group work. Group work may be introduced into classroom music lessons gradually. Those activities which suggest group work may also be managed as whole class activities.

Teaching songs

We hope that teachers will lead the singing with their own voice, particularly with younger children. But in all instances we have assumed that the teacher will use the CD.

If you feel confident, teach yourself a song using the CD and then teach it to the children.

To rehearse songs with your class without the CD, you might:

- sing the melody without the words, to lah or dee;
- chant the rhythm of the words;
- sing the song line by line for the children to copy.

Teachers' videoclips

There are seventeen videoclips on the CD-ROM that demonstrate useful teaching techniques to use in class music lessons.

Clip	Contents
T 01	The Music Express Song
T 02	Teaching a song line by line
T 03	Demonstrating pitch with hand
T 04	Starting together: speed and starting note
T 05	Internalising
T 06	Conducting with a score
T 07	Conducting getting louder
T 08	Inventing vocal ostinatos
T 09	Dividing a class into groups
T 10	Conducting start and stop
T 11	Building layers of sound
T 12	Playing a drone accompaniment
T 13	Recognising a word rhythm
T 14	Allocating accompaniment instruments
T 15	Conducting instrumental groups
T 16	Helping to perform a steady beat
T 17	Putting instruments away

Ongoing skills

'Ongoing skills' are identified by the QCA scheme of work as those skills which need to be continually developed and revisited. This is in addition to the activities in the six units. The QCA suggests that learning may take place as the opportunity arises throughout the school week, eg in short 5-minute sessions.

Music Express does not include a separate Ongoing skills unit, but addresses the skills throughout its activities. When using *Music Express* as a scheme, you will be fulfilling the learning objectives and outcomes of the QCA Ongoing skills unit.

If you teach music in one weekly lesson, as opposed to three shorter lessons, you may like to select activities from *Music Express* for supplementary 5-minute activities. By doing this, you will reinforce more regularly the development of the musical skills identified by the QCA.

Extension and future learning

A & C Black website

Music Express provides all the resources you will need for teaching a year of music. We hope, however, that you will use other songs and activities to ring the changes in subsequent years or to link with other National Curriculum subjects.

The website www.acblack.com/musicexpress lists the *Music Express* activities that were drawn from or inspired by other A & C Black books, and links to other books that will supplement the activities in *Music Express*.

SOUNDS ALL AROUND

1 **Sing *Sound song* to focus listening and to recognise a variety of sounds**

- Listen to *Sound song* together *(track 1a)*. What sounds can the children hear through their classroom window during the listening gaps? List the sound sources together *(eg voices, wind, bus, door, machine)* and describe the sounds *(eg quiet, loud, long, short, patterns of sounds)*.

- Teach the song by asking the children to echo-sing each line *(track 1b)*:

Sounds we hear,   Sounds we hear,
Through the window,   Through the window,
Far and near,   Far and near,
Soft and still,   Soft and still,
High and low,   High and low,
Loud and clear,   Loud and clear,

Listen ...
Listen ...
Listen ...
Listen. ...

- Sing the song again (with or without the CD), focusing the children's listening on the sounds farthest away. What did they hear this time?

- Sing again, noticing the nearest sounds.

Teaching tip
- Ask children who have difficulty focusing their listening to listen out for a specific sound, and raise their hand when they hear it, so that you can check.

Teaching tip
- Echo-singing is a useful method for teaching a song. You sing a line and the children copy, sing the next line and so on.

2 **Sing *Hands can hold* to make a variety of sounds using hands**

- All listen to the CD to familiarise yourselves with the song. Ask the children what hand sound is made at the end of each verse. *(Clap.)*

- Listen again. Can the children say how the accompaniment sounds are made? *(All the sounds are made with hands.)*

- Sing the song without the CD. All join in with the actions. Invite a child to make a new hand sound after the first verse, eg rubbing palms. Everyone copies the hand sound after the second verse.

Hands can hold and hands can *squeeze*,
Hands can rest upon your *knees*,
Hands can clap and hands can *shake*,
What kind of sound can your hands *make*?

  (Child makes a hand sound.)

Hands can hold and hands can *squeeze*,
Hands can rest upon our *knees*,
Hands can clap and hands can *shake*,
This is the sound which our hands make.

  (All copy the hand sound.)

3 **Create a piece of hand music using the *Sounds handy* score**

- Show the class the *Sounds handy* score and ask individual children to demonstrate each sound represented. How many of these sounds did the children find when they sang *Hands can hold*? Are there any new ones?

- To make a piece of hand music, point to each picture for a few seconds. The children perform each sound as you point to it. Practise a few times so that the children all learn to watch and change sounds together.

- Change the sequence of sounds by pointing to the pictures in a different order.

- Invite a child to conduct a new piece of *Sounds handy* music.

Sounds handy score

clap

rub

flick

click

tap

scratch

shake

tap nails

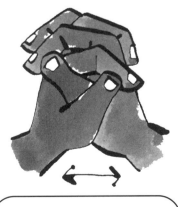

pop

Music Express Year 1 © A & C Black 2002
www.acblack.com/musicexpress

SOUNDS UNUSUAL

1 Sing *Sound song* adding vocal sounds and body percussion

- Sing *Sound song* to these new words, inviting children by name to contribute a sound each in the listening gaps. They may use their voices, hands and bodies (yawn, squeak, click, stamp, stroke, etc):

  Sounds we hear,   Sounds we hear,
  When we make them,   When we make them,
  Far and near,   Far and near,
  Soft and still,   Soft and still,
  High and low,   High and low,
  Loud and clear,   Loud and clear,

  Listen to Bobbie ...
  Listen to Sanjay ...
  Listen to Alice ...
  Listen to Sam. ...

- Repeat the song several times so the children make and hear a variety of sounds. Discuss each person's sound. Was it:

  – loud, quiet, squeaky, long, short, smooth, happy, sad, angry, scary?

2 Play the *Sound song* listening game to identify sound sources

- Invite a volunteer to hide behind a screen while you sing the song. The volunteer makes one of the sounds explored in activity 1 during the listening gaps. Can the others say how the sound is being made?

- Place a set of unusual sound sources in a large box. It might include any of those pictured below.

- Choose a child to select and secretly make a sound inside the box, out of sight of the class. Can the others say which object made the sound?

Teaching tips

- Place the sound box in a music corner where pairs of children can play the game. Change the contents frequently.

- Copy *Sounds menu* onto a computer or onto a cassette, which the children can access easily to listen to again on their own.

3 Listen to *Sounds menu* to identify sound sources

- Ask the children to say what each of the sounds in the music is being made by.

  (Microwave, dripping tap, toaster, bottle cork, cutlery drawer, steam iron, washing machine, kettle, water draining away, frying pan.)

CHOOSE AN INSTRUMENT

1 **Sing *Choose an instrument* to explore the sounds of percussion instruments**

- All listen to the CD to familiarise yourselves with the song.

- All sit in a circle with a small selection of percussion instruments in the centre. A beanbag is passed round while you sing the first verse. Whoever holds the beanbag at the end chooses an instrument and plays it freely while you sing the second verse.

Choose an instrument you can play,
You can play, you can play,
Choose an instrument you can play,
What's your favourite?

You can play the tambourine,
Tambourine, tambourine,
You can play the tambourine,
That's your favourite.

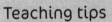

Teaching tips
- Encourage the children to participate by mimicking the action of playing the chosen instrument while you sing.
- The children may play rhythmically or freely; either is acceptable and will help build their experience of handling and playing instruments.

2 **Sing *Listen to the east* to demonstrate different ways of playing instruments**

- All listen to the CD to familiarise yourselves with the song.

- Select four or five different instruments to demonstrate. All sing the song. You play one of the instruments in the gaps after lines 1, 2 and 4, eg you might tap a tambour with fingertips. Ask the children to name the instrument and describe how you are playing it.

Listen to the east, _____
Listen to the west, _____
Listen to the sound and play
The listening test. _____

- Repeat this until each instrument has been played in a variety of ways, eg a tambourine may be tapped, shaken, scraped with a fingernail, etc. Discuss the sounds produced by the methods of play. Are they loud, quiet, fast, slow ...?

3 **Play the *Listen to the east* game to discriminate between sounds made by playing instruments in different ways**

- Use two sets of the five percussion instruments. Place one of each behind a screen. Keep the original five in view. All sing the song and you play one of the hidden instruments:

Listen to the east, _____ *(etc)*

- Can the children identify and name the instrument which is making the sound, and say how it is being played? *(Use the visible set as reference.)*

Invite one of the children to play, using the same playing technique, as you all sing the answering verse:

Play it to the east, _____
Play it to the west, _____
Play us all the instrument
That sounds the best. _____

Teaching tips
- The song may be chanted to allow you to concentrate on playing the instruments.
- Invite individuals to play, rather than demonstrating all of the instruments yourself.

STOP START SOUNDS

1 **Sing *Choose an instrument*
to develop skill handling
classroom instruments**

- All sit in a circle with a large selection of
instruments in the centre. A beanbag is
passed round while you sing the first verse.
Whoever holds the beanbag at the end,
chooses an instrument. They respond to
the directions to play or stop in the second
verse, finding a way to control their
instrument effectively:

Choose an instrument you can play,
You can play, you can play,
Choose an instrument you can play,
What's your favourite?

You can play and play and STOP,
Play and STOP, play and STOP,
You can play and play and STOP,
Play and STOP it.

- Repeat the game, inviting a second child to
choose and play.

> ## Teaching tip
> - Some instruments are easier to stop
> than others, as the children will find
> out. Ask them to invent a special
> way of holding the instrument to
> silence it, eg hold tambourine
> vertically, rest jingle bells on a knee,
> touch a chime bar with a fingertip.

Traffic light template

2 **Play *Traffic lights* to conduct
starting and stopping**

- Give each child a small hand-held percussion
instrument. Hold up the green side of the
traffic light (*photocopiable template above*)
as a signal to start playing. When you turn
the signal to red all stop.

- Practise several times, varying the length of
time you show each signal. Can the children
all follow the signals and control their
instruments when you change to stop?

- Invite a child to be the traffic controller.

3 **Listen to the story and add sounds to
*The big blue jeep and the little white trike***

- All listen to the CD. Encourage the children to listen carefully to the
sounds which the jeep and the trike make.

- On a second listening, invite the children to join in making the sound
effects with voices and hands.

> ## Teaching tip
> - Sit children who find it difficult
> to follow the signals near to
> the conductor so that they
> are not distracted.

SOUNDS ON THE MOVE

1 **Sing *The wheels on the bus* to explore expressive ways of using the voice**

- Listen to the CD. All join in singing the song as it becomes familiar:

  The wheels on the bus go round and round,
  Round and round, round and round,
  The wheels on the bus go round and round,
     All day long.
  The bell on the bus goes ding ding ding ...
  The babies on the bus all clap their hands ...

- Now ask the children to suggest ways of changing their voices to reflect the words of the song, eg

  - wheels verse: sing gradually faster then slower;

  - bell verse: sing in high tinkly voices;

  - babies verse: sing in babies' voices.

- Ask the children to suggest more ideas for verses, and sing in voices which match, eg bus conductor, horn, aliens, etc *(the children will have their own fantastical ideas)*.

Teaching tips
- Choose the groups carefully to mix more confident with less confident children. Encourage all to think carefully how to make the best musical effect with their sounds.
- Use hand signals or the traffic light signal to conduct the players, showing them when to start and stop.

2 **Perform *The wheels on the bus* with instruments**

- Ask the children to suggest instrumental sounds to reflect the words of the song, eg

  - wheels verse: scrape a guiro continuously;

  - bell verse: triangle on 'ting ting ting';

  - babies verse: tap claves lightly on 'clap their hands'.

- Divide the class into three groups and allocate the chosen instruments to each.

- Practise each verse, giving each group a turn to play their sounds, while the others sing the song and keep their instruments silent.

- Perform the song with the instrumental accompaniments from each group.

3 **Listen to *The big blue jeep and the little white trike* and add instrumental sounds**

- Play the CD to remind the children of the story.

- Select two small groups. Decide together on an instrumental sound to represent the jeep - its engine and large wheels; decide on an instrumental sound to represent the trike - its bell and small wheels. Distribute the respective instruments to the groups.

- Discuss and practise the way the instruments might be played to give an effective impression of the two characters: the fast, angry, noisy jeep, and the slow, steady, polite trike.

- Select a third, fourth and fifth group to make the vocal sounds for the jeep's mishaps: the muddy puddle, refuelling, and burst tyre. Practise these.

- Now tell the story entirely in sound. Using the traffic light signal, direct the groups to stop and start. The trike group begins and continues to play throughout. The jeep group stops and starts, and the other three groups make their sounds in turn as directed.

SOUNDS IN THE CITY

1 Listen to the expressive use of music in *The little train of the Caipira*

- Explain that the children are going to hear some music which describes a train journey. After listening, ask the children what they imagine happened on the train journey, eg

  – did the train move slowly, quickly, up hill or down?

  – what might they have seen from the train windows?

- How does the music describe the things they imagine?

- As they listen to the music again, the children may join in with vocal sounds (and actions), adding them to those which already describe the events of the journey.

Background information

The little train of the Caipira was composed by Villa Lobos (1897-1959). The music describes travelling through the Brazilian mountains on a steam train.

2 Use the *City sounds* score to explore playing city sounds

p15

- Revise the vocal, body and instrumental sounds the children have found to represent the bus, train, jeep and trike.

- Show the children *City sounds score*. Do they recognise any of the vehicles? Remind the children of the sounds they found for each. Talk about other sounds they might hear if they were walking along this city road, eg footsteps, voices, pedestrian crossings. Use voices, hands, and body percussion to represent them.

- Divide into small groups - one for each vehicle, and a pedestrians group. Conduct the groups by moving a pointer along the road in the score. Each group plays as the pointer moves over the picture of their vehicle. The pedestrian group perform their sounds all through.

Teaching tip

Invite individual children to contribute their ideas and perform their sounds for the class to copy.

3 Listen to *Sing a song of people* and add *City sounds*

- All listen to track 10, then ask the children where they think the song is set. *(In the city.)*

  What sounds tell them this? *(Traffic, footsteps on pavements, voices, bus, van, train, cars.)*

- Review the vocal and instrumental sounds found for *City sounds* (activity 2). Discuss how these sounds might be added during the instrumental sections of *Sing a song of people*, eg using the score to conduct groups of players making city sounds.

  Play track 11 and conduct the groups by moving the pointer along all or part of the score during the instrumental sections of the song.

- Invite a child to conduct.

City sounds score

The long and the short of it
Exploring duration

SOUNDS LONG OR SHORT

1 **Sing *Some sounds are short* to explore making long and short vocal sounds**

- All listen to the CD to familiarise yourselves with the song.

- All sit in a circle. A beanbag is passed round while you sing the first verse. Whoever holds the beanbag at the end of the first verse makes a long or a short sound with their voice:

    Some sounds are short,
    Some sounds are long,
    Which sound will you make
    After this song?
    (Child makes a long or short vocal sound.)

The others say whether the sound was long or short, then you sing:

    Some sounds are short,
    Some sounds are long,
    You made a (short/long) sound
    After the song.
    (All copy the vocal sound.)

- Play again.

3 **Play the *Fireworks bingo* game to focus listening**

- Make enough sets of *Firework bingo* cards to give one set each to pairs or small groups of children. Each pair or group shuffles them.

- Listen to track 14. The children put the cards into the order of the fireworks they hear. They may need to listen more than once.

    When they have ordered their cards, check their answers. *(Answer: 3, 2, 6, 1, 5, 4.)*

- Invite one pair or group to perform the six firework vocal sounds and actions in a secret order of their choosing. The others order their cards to match.

2 **Listen to fireworks and create firework sound effects with reference to *Fireworks bingo***

- As a class match the firework pictures to the firework sounds on track 13. *(The CD matches the numbered order.)* Label them.

- Talk about the sounds each firework makes:
    - are they long? short? a sequence of long and short sounds?

- Ask them to discover ways of using their voices to make the sounds of each firework.

- Find actions to accompany the firework sounds, eg
    - rocket: crouch, stretch to standing and clap;
    - catherine wheel: circle hand quickly;
    - sparkler: wiggle fingers.

- Invite a child to point to each firework on the photocopiable in an order of their own choosing. The others respond in sound and action.

- Give other children a turn to conduct.

Teaching tip
Invite individual children to contribute their ideas and perform their sounds and actions for the class to copy.

Fireworks bingo

1

2

3

4

5

6

Music Express Year 1 © A & C Black 2002
www.acblack.com/musicexpress

FIREWORK NIGHT

1 Explore instruments to make firework sounds

- Revise the firework sounds and actions from Lesson 1 for catherine wheel, banger and rocket. Were the sounds they made long or short? Were they a sequence of long and short?

- Make available a large selection of tuned and untuned percussion instruments. Divide the class into three groups.

  Allocate the three firework cards, and ask the groups to be thinking of appropriate instrumental sounds to match their card. Invite each group to select their percussion. Allow time and space for the class to experiment with their ideas.

- Ask each group to play to the others. As a class, discuss the choices. Are the sounds appropriately long, short or an effective sequence?

Teaching tip

- Dividing into groups: if space allows, ask the groups to move as far apart as they can so that they may focus more closely on their own work.

2 Add actions and vocal sounds to the song, *It's bonfire night*

- All listen to the CD and join in with the chorus as it becomes familiar:

  It's bonfire night,
  It's bonfire night,
  It's bonfire night,
  And the sky is bright.

- Together, place the three firework cards in the order of the verses and review the actions and vocal sounds from Lesson 1. Add them to the appropriate verse as the CD plays, eg

  See the catherine wheel (action)
  Listen to the sound (woooooooooooooosh)
  See the catherine wheel (action)
  Listen to the sound (woooooooooooooosh).

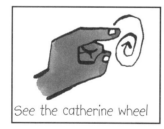

See the catherine wheel

Listen to the sound ----

See the catherine wheel

Listen to the sound ----

3 Add instrumental sounds to *It's bonfire night*

- As the CD plays, the three groups from activity 1 add their instrumental sounds to the appropriate verses, while everyone else adds actions and vocal sounds (*use the firework cards again as a visual reminder of the order*).

See the catherine wheel

Listen to the sound ----

See the catherine wheel

Listen to the sound ----

SOUND WAVES

1 Listen to the duration of sounds made by different instruments in the song, *Fade or float?*

- Listen to the song. The children determine whether the instrument played after each verse makes a long or a short sound.

- Next, show the children a selection of instruments including a cymbal, tambour, woodblock and chime bar. Invite individual children to take turns to play a single sound on each instrument. Which sounds faded? Which floated?

Teaching tips

- The natural property of an instrument will produce a long or a short sound, eg metal, more often than wood or skin, produces a long sound.

- Check that the instrument is held in such a way that it may vibrate freely.

- Note that different techniques of striking the instrument will result in different lengths of sound, eg a cymbal will make a short sound if the beater is not allowed to bounce off instantly. You may need to discuss this.

2 Sing *Fade or float?* and predict the duration of sounds made by different instruments

- All sit in a circle with a large selection of instruments in the centre. A rubber-headed beater is passed round the circle while you sing the song:

Take a beater, strike a note,
Strike a note, strike a note,
In the air the sound might float –
Or fade quickly.

Whoever holds the beater at the end chooses an instrument and predicts whether the sound will be long or short.

The child then strikes the instrument once to check whether the prediction is correct.

3 Use the rhyme, *Bubble*, to perform long and short vocal and body sounds, and whole body movements

- Say the rhyme together, making the fingerplay actions, the long vocal sound and short 'pop':

Here's the soap to wash your hands,
(rub hands together as if washing)

Now blow a big bubble – Foooooooo,
(blow an imaginary bubble)

And see where it lands –
(follow path of 'bubble' with fingertip making a long sound with the voice, then say –)

POP!

- Using bubble mixture, blow a stream of bubbles. Ask the children each to focus on one bubble, and follow its course with a fingertip in the air and a long vocal sound until it pops.

- Invite a small group to move lightly and smoothly as the bubbles float in the air, stopping and 'freezing' when the last one has popped. The other children make long vocal sounds until the last bubble pops.

POP, RIPPLE AND FREEZE

1 **Explore making long and short instrumental sounds then play the *Bubble* game to focus listening**

* All sit in a circle with a selection of instruments in the centre. Find ways to play a long sound and a short sound on each instrument, eg

  – rub the skin of a tambour with a fingertip, then tap it;

  – swirl a maraca, then tap in the palm of the hand;

  – tap a cymbal and let it ring, then tap again pinching the edge to stop the sound quickly.

* Remind the children of the *Bubble* rhyme (lesson 3).

  Invite one child to take an instrument behind a screen.

  The others say the rhyme with the actions but pause after 'see where it lands'. Invite them to close their eyes.

  The hidden child makes a long sound on the instrument then a short 'pop'. The others trace the sound in the air with a fingertip until they hear the short 'pop' sound when they rest fingertips on the floor.

2 **Listen to *Rippling rhythm* to identify long and short sounds heard together**

* As they listen to the CD, the children mark the sound of the water bubbles by wiggling their fingers continuously whenever they hear them. Do they make a long or a short sound? *(Long.)*

* Listen again, wiggling fingers during the bubble sections. Can the children name the instrument which plays short sounds at the same time as the bubbles? *(Piano.)* Ask half the class to wiggle their fingers for the bubbles, and the other half to tap their noses with a fingertip for the short piano sounds as you all listen again.

* Ask the class to nod their heads from side to side when they hear the tick tock sounds. Are they long or short? *(Short.)* Can they name the instrument which plays at the same time as the tick tocking? *(Violin.)* Does it play a long or a short sound? *(Long.)*

  Ask half the class to mark the violin sound with a long, smooth action, eg draw an imaginary bow across a violin.

* Listen again, marking the long and short sound combinations with the actions.

Background information

* *Rippling rhythm* is a piece of early 20th century dance band music.

3 **Listen to *Ho! Jack Frost* and join in with words and actions**

* All listen to the CD, joining in with the repeated line, 'Ho! Jack Frost.'

* Encourage the children to sing 'Ho! Jack Frost', making the words short and crisp. To emphasise this they might add short actions, eg jerk arms and hands as though tossing ice crystals.

LONG WINTER, COLD SNAP

1 **Sing *Ho! Jack Frost* and listen to long and short sounds in the accompaniment**

- All listen to the CD and learn to sing the whole song:

Who turns the trees all silver white? Ho! Jack Frost.
Who helps us make a slippery slide? Ho! Jack Frost.
Who comes so silent through the night
   and scatters crystals sharp and bright?
Who paints the windows snowy white? Ho! Jack Frost.

- Listen again and ask which percussion instrument is playing on the words, 'Ho! Jack Frost'? *(Drum.)* Does it play long or short sounds? *(Short.)*

- Listen again and ask which instruments make long sounds during the four questions. *(Triangle and chime bars.)*

  Ask which questions the triangle accompanies. *(First, second, fourth.)* Which question do the chime bars accompany? *(Third.)*

- Discuss the choice of instruments. Are they an effective accompaniment to the words?

> **Teaching tips**
> • Say the words line by line, asking the children to repeat them after you. Listen to the CD, and all join in as the melody becomes familiar.
>
> • The children may need to listen several times to answer these questions.

2 **Choose long and short sounds to accompany *Ho! Jack Frost***

- As a class, find four long sounds from a selection of instruments or soundmakers to accompany each of the four questions and short sounds to accompany 'Ho! Jack Frost', eg

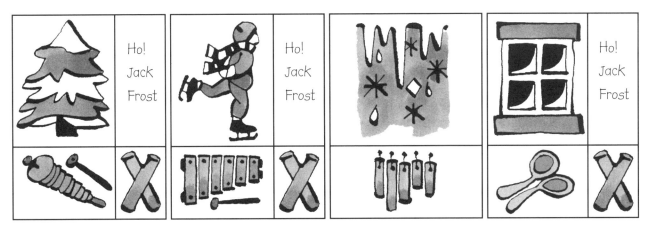

- Select children to play the instrumental sounds, and all rehearse singing the song with the new percussion accompaniment. Swap players.

3 **Listen and move to the song, *Coming down*, singing the repeated lines**

- Before listening, remind the children of the actions they found for catherine wheels. How might they move to describe raindrops falling, snowflakes drifting, cracking ice? Will these movements be long and smooth, short and spiky?

- Listen to the song. In the instrumental repeat of each verse, move in ways which describe the verse words.

- Listen and move again, joining in singing the two repeated lines of the verses.

MOVING INTO WINTER

1 **Sing *Coming down* and perform it with movements**

- All listen to the CD to learn the whole song. Ensure that the children are familiar with all the words and confident singing the melody:

  Watching fireworks, catherine wheels spin round,
  Sparks fall to the ground,
  They go spinning and flying around,
  They go spinning and flying around.

  Falling raindrops, make a tiny sound,
  As they hit the ground,
  They come pittering, pattering down,
  They come pittering, pattering down.

  Catching snowflakes before they touch the ground.
  Before they touch the ground,
  They go swirling and whirling around,
  They go swirling and whirling around.

  Frozen puddles, on the icy ground,
  Hear the crackling sound,
  As we step on the ice all around,
  As we step on the ice all around.

- All sing the song with the CD. Ask a small group to perform the movements explored earlier as each verse is repeated.

2 **Choose and order sounds to represent each of the *Sounds of winter* pictures**

- Divide the class into four groups with space in which to rehearse. Give each a set of the four pictures and a wide selection of instruments.

- As a class discuss sounds to represent the pictures – will they be long, short, sequences or combinations of both?

- The groups choose and rehearse the sounds for each picture, then appoint a conductor. The conductor orders the cards and indicates when to start and stop playing by pointing to the cards in turn.

- Each group performs their sounds to the rest of the class, keeping the order secret. Can the other groups identify the order and put their card set in sequence as they listen?

  Do the chosen sounds effectively represent the pictures? Do they contrast well with each other?

  Which group created the most effective rain sounds? snow? fireworks? ice?

> ### Teaching tip
> - Use the *Sounds of winter* pictures to help the children remember the order of the verses.

3 **Perform *Coming down* and *Sounds of winter***

- Each group from activity 2 is allocated the card they most effectively represented and rehearses singing their verse from *Coming down*, followed by playing their descriptive sounds as the music is repeated (*optional backing track 20*).

- Finally, perform the whole song, with the groups contributing their sung verse and instrumental verse in turn.

- Each group might choose one or two children to interpret the music in the movements they found earlier.

Sounds of winter

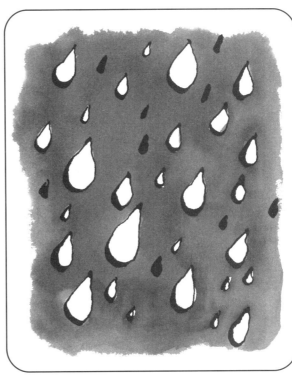

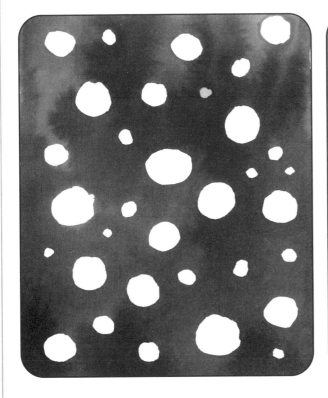

Music Express Year 1 © A & C Black 2002
www.acblack.com/musicexpress

MOVE YOURSELF

1 **Move to the beat of the song, *Pinocchio*** 21-22))

• All listen to track 21 and join in with actions to the steady beat:

Here   is   what   my   arm   can   do ...

My name is Pinocchio. I am in a puppet show,
I can move my wooden arm, it goes like this.
Here is what my arm can do, see if you can do it too,
Here is what my arm can do, it goes like this.

My name is Pinocchio. I am in a puppet show,
I can nod my wooden head ...

I can tap my wooden feet ...

• Explain that these actions are performed to the beat of the song. Play track 22. Sing again, all clapping hands to the beat:

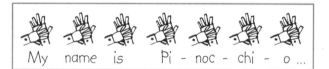

My   name   is   Pi - noc - chi - o ...

2 **Respond to *Raga abhogi* and *Country dance* in movement** 23-24))

• Invite the children to draw shapes freely in the air with their hands and fingers as they listen to *Raga abhogi.* Can they describe how their hands move to match the music? (*With slow, smooth, changing shapes.*)

• Now respond to *Country dance.* What do they notice about the movements this time? (*Many will have moved to the beat.*)

• Explain that in *Raga abhogi* there is no steady beat, while in *Country dance* there is a strong, steady beat. Play *Country dance* again, asking the children to tap the beat on their knees, (hands together, or alternately).

Background information

• *Raga Abhogi* is from India and is played by flute and tamboura.

• *Country dance* comes from *The Water Music* by Handel (1685 - 1759).

3 **Sing *Okki-tokki-unga* with actions on the beat** 25))

• All listen to the CD and sing the song with the suggested actions which mark the beat and tell the story of an Inuit boy who goes fishing:

– Chorus: paddle to one side then the other

– Vs 1: peer to one side then the other

– Vs 2: cast net to one side then the other

– Vs 3: cast net to one side then the other

– Last chorus: paddle slowly and wearily home.

Ch   Okki-tokki-unga,
      Okki-tokki-unga,
      Hey, Missa day, Missa doh,
      Missa day. *(Repeat)*

Vs1-3 Hexa cola misha woni,
       Hexa cola misha woni,
       Hexa cola misha woni.

Ch   Okki - tokki - un - ga   Okki - tokki - un - ga

Vs 1 He - xa cola misha   wo — ni

Vs 2 He - xa cola misha   wo — ni

Vs 3 He - xa cola misha   wo — ni

Ch   Okki - tokki - un - ga   Okki - tokki - un - ga

FOLLOW ME

1 **Sing *Pinocchio's band*, accompanying it with instruments played on the beat**

- Give five or six children drums and choose one of them to be 'Pinocchio'. Ask this child to play the drum to the beat you clapped in Lesson 1 as you all sing. The other drummers join in after 'See if you can do it too' and continue until the end of the verse.

(one drummer)
My name is Pinocchio. I am in a music show,
I can play a magic drum, it goes like this.
Here is what my drum can do, see if you can do it too,
(all drummers)
Dum dum dum dum dum dum dum, it goes like this.

- Repeat with other groups of players and different instruments, eg woodblocks, tambourines.

2 **Play the *Get on board* game to move to beats at changing speeds**

- Everyone stands in a large circle. Tell the children that in this game you are the 'train driver'. Begin tapping a constant beat on a cowbell and step in time to it *(reference track 26a)*. The children join in, stepping on the spot. As you, the train driver, start to move around inside the circle, add this chant:

Get on board, Get on board ...

which leads to inviting a child to join the train behind you:

Get on board, Ish - rat,
Ish - rat, Ish - rat ...

Invite another child to join on and continue the game until the train is as long as you want.

- Let individual children be the train driver while you conduct the beat using the cowbell. Encourage all to join in with the chant.

- When the game is familiar you can alter the speed of the beat: gradually speeding up or slowing down the cowbell beat as though the train were speeding up or slowing down. Can the children follow the beat and step in time? *(Reference track 26b.)*

3 **Listen to *Bransle de chevaux* to identify the beat**

- Ask the children to tap the beat of the music on their knees as they listen to the CD or watch the videoclip.

- Did the beat stay the same all the way through the music or did it change speed?

(It changed speed; it was faster each time the dance was repeated.)

Background information

- *Bransle de chevaux* is an old French dance. It was the most popular dance of its time performed in both city court and country festival.

3rd
Feel the pulse
Exploring pulse and rhythm

BEAT AND RHYTHM

1 Sing *I hear thunder* and mark the beat with clapping

- All listen to the CD and echo-sing each line of the song together. As you sing, clap the beat:

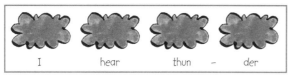

| I | hear | thun | – | der |

I hear thunder
Hark don't you?
Pitter patter raindrops
I'm wet through!

I hear thunder
Hark don't you?
Pitter patter raindrops
So are you!

- Sing the whole song together.

Teaching tip
- Notice the children who are clapping the beat when asked to clap the rhythm, and vice versa. Give them plenty of opportunity to practise this, using the picture chart.

2 Sing *I hear thunder* to recognise the difference between beat and rhythm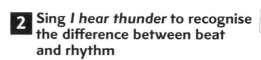

- Show the children *Thunder beats* and ask them to clap as you point to the 'cloud' beats and sing the song. Repeat until this is secure. (Videoclip 3.)

- Clap the word rhythm of 'pitter patter raindrops' (without saying the words themselves).

| (pit – ter | pat – ter | rain | – | drops) |

Can the children say which words you clapped? (Videoclip 4.)

Compare the clapped word rhythm with the clapped beat. How are they different? (*The rhythm changes – it makes a pattern of long and short; the beat stays the same – the claps are spaced evenly.*) (Videoclip 5.)

- Show the children *Thunder rhythms*. All listen to track 29 and echo-clap the word rhythms for each line.

Listen to track 30 and clap the rhythm of the whole song. Ask the children to clap again as you point to the symbols. (Videoclip 6.)

When are the beat and the rhythm the same?

(*The line 'I hear thunder'.*)

Which word rhythm patterns are the same?

(*Lines 2 and 4*)

3 Sing *Okki-tokki-unga* to combine beat and rhythm

- Revise singing the chorus with the paddling actions to the beat (*reference track 31a*).

- Ask the children to clap the word rhythm of the chorus as you sing it together (*reference track 31b*):

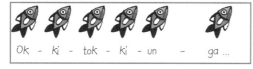

| Ok – ki – tok – ki – un | – | ga ... |

- Perform the song like this. All sing the chorus while:

  – half the class paddles in time with the beat;

  – half the class claps the rhythm of the words.

Repeat, vice versa. (*Reference track 31c.*)

Thunder beats

Repeat each line

Thunder rhythms

Feel the pulse
Exploring pulse and rhythm

DRUM BEATS AND RHYTHMS

1 **Sing *This old man* and clap the beat and rhythm**

- Ask the children, as they listen to track 32, to clap the beat of the song:

This old man,
He played one ...

- Sing the song together and clap the beat:

> This old man,
> He played one,
> He played nick nack
> On my drum with a
> Nick nack paddy wack
> Give the dog a bone,
> This old man came
> Rolling home.

- All listen to track 33. Ask the children to say whether they hear the beat or the word rhythms played. *(The word rhythms.)*

- Clap and say the rhythm of each line of words one line at a time, inviting the children to echo you. *(Track 34.)*

- Practise each line separately several times – with the words, then without.

  Clap a line of words. Can the children identify it? *(Some have the same pattern: lines 1 and 2, 3 and 7.)*

Teaching tips

- When clapping the rhythm of a line together or performing in two groups, bring everyone in together with a steady count, eg 1 2 3 4.

- The words are given in the photocopiable as a reference, but it is always helpful to say the words as they are clapped – out loud then silently.

- Help the ostinato group to keep in time with each other by counting them in and tapping along with them until the rhythm is secure.

2 **Accompany *This old man* with word rhythms**

- Show the children the photocopiable, *The old man's drum.* As a class, tap the rhythm of one line on your knees repeatedly as though on a drum *(track 35).* Repeat with the other lines.

- Invite a child to select and demonstrate one of the rhythms on a drum. The others tap the rhythm on their knees.

  Select a small group of children. Ask them to say and tap the selected line on their knees repeatedly until you signal them to stop.

  The other children sing the song to the 'drum' accompaniment. *(This is called an ostinato and may be heard on track 36.)*

Nick nack pad-dy wack...
This old man ... etc

- Invite another child to select and demonstrate another drum rhythm from the photocopiable.

  Select another group of children to say and tap the new drum rhythm while the others sing, and so on.

3 **Sing *Clap your hands* with action patterns**

- All listen to the CD, joining in singing as it becomes familiar:

> Clap your hands and wiggle your fingers,
> Clap your hands and wiggle your fingers,
> Clap your hands and wiggle your fingers,
> Now we've made a pattern.

- Perform this pattern of actions as you all sing again:

Clap your hands and wiggle your fin - gers ...

- You or a child suggests how the pattern might be varied, eg

Clap your hands and wiggle your fin - gers ...

- Invite further variations, and different actions.

The old man's drum

| 1 | 2 | 3 | 4 |

1. Ref: This   old   man

2. He   played   nick   nack

3. On   my   drum   with   a

4. Nick   nack   pad - dy   wack

5. Give   the   dog   a   bone

Music Express Year 1 © A & C Black 2002
www.acblack.com/musicexpress

Feel the pulse
Exploring pulse and rhythm

READ THE RHYTHM

1 Sing *This old man* and improvise rhythm patterns

- Show the children the photocopiable, *The old man's drum.* Show them that each rhythm fits into a count of four beats. Tell the class that they are going to make up their own rhythm patterns to fit into a count of four beats.

- Sit the children in a circle and sing the song. Instead of singing the words 'nick nack paddy wack', signal four silent beats with four hand waves - then continue the song *(reference track 38).*

This old man,
He played one,
He played nick nack
On my drum with a–

Give the dog a bone,
This old man came
Rolling home.

- When this is secure, sing the song and pass a hand drum around the circle.

On the word 'drum', the child who is holding the instrument keeps it and prepares to play. As before, the singers stop singing. They listen as the drummer contributes a rhythm which fits into the four-beat gap, then resume *(track 38).*

2 Write and read simple rhythms using the *Clap and wiggle* score

- Remind the children of the rhythm patterns they suggested for *Clap your hands.* Perform some of them.

- Select one of the rhythm patterns and ask the children to suggest two percussion instruments to play the pattern, eg claves and tambourine:

Clap your hands and wiggle your fin - gers ...

- Show the children the *Clap and wiggle* score (chart 1) which indicates the beat (boxes) and the rhythm (filled boxes). Select two children to play the rhythm pattern while everyone sings the song. *(Reference track 39.)*

- Choose one of the new action patterns suggested by the children and agree on two instruments to play it. Invite a child to mark the new rhythm pattern on the blank score by filling in or marking the appropriate boxes, eg

Stamp your feet and tap your knees

Perform the pattern from the score as you sing the song. Repeat with other patterns.

3 Mark the beat of *A dragon's very fierce*

- Invite the children to tap the beat on their knees, as they listen to the recording of the chant:

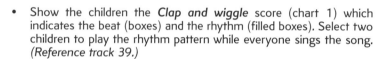

Oh, a dragon's very fierce   A ...

- Can the children think of other ways of marking the beat, eg stamping feet, moving claws, swishing tail, playing a scraper or drum? Accompany the recording with their suggestions. Make an extra-large foot stamp on the last beat.

Clap and wiggle score

Score 1

1	2	3	4
V		V	V
Clap	your	hands	and

⋀⋀⋀		⋀⋀⋀	⋀⋀⋀
wiggle	your	fin	- gers

Blank score

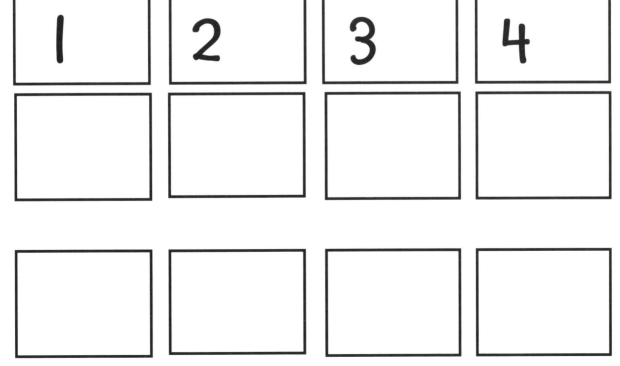

DRAGON BEATS

1 Chant *A dragon's very fierce* and add actions and sounds

- Listen to the CD together to familiarise yourselves with the words of the chant:

Oh, a dragon's very fierce,
A dragon's very tough,
And when he breathes out orange fire
The smoke comes out in puffs!
His scales are shining green,
They make a rattling sound,
His feet go stomp,
His teeth go chomp,
His tail thumps on the ground. *

When this is secure, add the actions and sounds suggested in the last lesson. Perform these to the beat of the chant.

Teaching tips

- Make sure that the drone players are holding the beaters correctly and bouncing them on the bars to produce a resonant sound.
- Encourage each player to hold two beaters and alternate left and right hands.
- Place the *Dragon score* in the music corner where individuals and pairs may work with it.

2 Create an accompaniment for *A dragon's very fierce*

- A small group accompany the chant with a drone (*the same notes played throughout*) on the beat (*track 41a*):

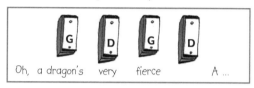

Oh, a dragon's	very	fierce	A ...

- A small group accompany the chant, playing a repeating rhythm pattern (ostinato) on percussion (*track 41b*):

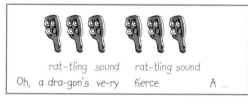

rat-tling sound   rat-tling sound
Oh, a dra-gon's ve-ry   fierce   A ...

- Invite individual children to choose sounds for single words, and play these on appropriate instruments, eg
  - scales - triangle
  - stomp - drum
  - chomp - scraper

Practise adding these individual sounds to the chant.

- Use the *Dragon score*, to conduct a performance of the piece (*track 41c*), pointing to the score to indicate when players should begin, eg
  - drone group starts,
  - ostinato group joins in,
  - the others say the chant and tap the steady beat, adding
  - individual instrumental sounds;
  - drone and ostinato group continue, getting gradually quieter until you indicate 'Stop'.

3 Perform *A dragon's very fierce*

- Record a performance of the chant, then listen together. Ask the children if they think they need to make any improvements or changes?
  - Did the drone group keep a steady beat?
  - Did the rhythm pattern (ostinato) group keep in time with the beat?
  - Could the poem be heard clearly?
- Make any necessary refinements, then perform to another class or in assembly.

Dragon score

HIGH LOW VOICES

1 **Sing *Five little froggies* to make actions to match pitch**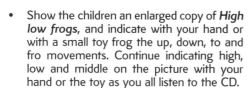

- Show the children an enlarged copy of *High low frogs*, and indicate with your hand or with a small toy frog the up, down, to and fro movements. Continue indicating high, low and middle on the picture with your hand or the toy as you all listen to the CD.

Five little froggies sitting on a well,

One leaned over and down she fell,

Froggies jump high,

Froggies jump low,

Four little froggies

Jumping to and fro.

- Sing the song together, all making actions with hands to show the pitch movement.

2 **Use high, medium and low voices in *Goldilocks and the three bears***

- Teach the children the three bears' responses. Encourage them to find their lowest voices for Big Bear's words, middle-pitched voices for Mama Bear's, and high voices for Baby Bear's.

Hey there, Big Bear, what d'you like for breakfast?
Cornflakes, rice cakes, Weetabix or what?

I like porridge! Give me porridge!
I like a lot of porridge in a great big pot!

Hey there, Mama Bear, what d'you like to sit in?
Arm chair, deck chair, rocking chair or what?

I like my chair, my sit-and-shut-your-eye chair,
My watch-the-world-go-by chair, I like my chair a lot.

Hey there, Baby Bear, what d'you like to sleep in?
Bath tub, coal bin, flower bed or what?

That's real easy! It's easy squeezy wheezy!
There's nothing in the world to beat my own small cot!

Hey there, three bears! What d'you think of Goldilocks?

BOOOOOOOOOO!

- Perform the chant together. You ask the questions and the class respond using the appropriate voices.

3 **Play the *Three bears* game to sing at different pitches**

- Show the class enlarged copies of the three bear cards opposite and invite a child to choose one. Sing a well-known song, eg *Twinkle twinkle little star*, in a pitch which matches the chosen bear card: high, low or medium.

- Repeat the game with the other cards and different songs.

- Change the cards during the song. Can the children respond instantly and change the pitch of their voices?

Photocopiable bear cards

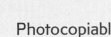

High low frogs

HIGH LOW - DO YOU KNOW?

Teaching tip

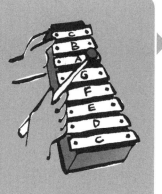

- Both *Slide song* and *Jack's game* may be played on a xylophone either by you or by a child.
- Support the xylophone for these activities in an upright position so that the long bars are near the floor, the short bars raised up. This shows a clear spatial relationship between high and low sounds.

2 Play *Jack's game* to recognise pitch movement

- Listen to the CD together. All mirror the pitch movement with your hands as you listen. Jack's game is played three times, and after each time the xylophone (Jack) is heard 'climbing' up, 'climbing' down, or 'hiding' in the middle. Ask the children to say which. *(Up, middle, down.)*

- All sing *Jack's song*. You or a child play the answer on a xylophone for the others to guess:

C D E F G A B C'
Is Jack climb-ing up the bean-stalk?

C' B A G F E D C
Is Jack climb-ing down the bean-stalk?

G G G G G G G
Is he hid - ing, keep -ing still?

Listen! *(Play line one, two or three again.)*

Ask the children to indicate their answers with hand signals *(climbing up, climbing down, hands over eyes)*. Play again.

1 Sing *Slide song* to practise moving pitch

- Listen to the CD together. As you listen, move your hand from low to high, step by step, sliding it down at the end, to give the children a visual indication of the way the pitch moves.

- Listen again. All crouch, rising little by little to full height, then sliding down to the floor at the end.

- Sing the song together with whole body or hand actions.

C C C   D D D
In the park,   there are stairs

E E E   F F F
Climb each one,   take great care

G G G   A A A
At the top,   it's your ride

B B B   C'   C
Hold on tight!   Sli--------de.

3 Listen to *Miss Mary Mac* to identify pitch movement

- Listen to the CD together. How does this melody move?

  – Does it go up? Down? Or does it stay in the same place? *(Each line moves up then stays in the same place.)*

  – Does it jump up or move by step? *(It moves by step.)*

- Ask the children to indicate the pitch movement with their hands as they listen again.

HIGH LOW MOVERS

1 Play *Jack's game* responding to pitch changes with movement

- Revise the song and game from Lesson 2, activity 2.

- Explain that now the xylophone will be hidden. The children listen to the hidden xylophone matching the pitch movement they hear with whole body actions: climbing up or down, or staying still.

- Play a sequence (without the song) of two or three pitch movements, eg Jack climbing up, staying hidden, climbing down. The children respond with the matching sequence of whole body actions.

Teaching tip

- Prepare a xylophone with the notes needed for Miss Mary Mac's melody (see illustration).

2 Add whole body actions to *Miss Mary Mac* and read *Mary Mac's score*

- Sing the song together *(with or without the CD).*

Miss Mary Mac Mac Mac
All dressed in black black black
With silver buttons buttons buttons
All down her back back back.

- Match the way the pitch of the melody moves with whole body actions:

Miss   Ma – ry   Mac   Mac   Mac

- Ask the children to say how many times they performed the same set of actions. *(Four times – once for each line of the song.)*

  Was the melody the same or different for each set of actions? *(The same.)*

- Show the children *Mary Mac's score* (Score 1). Sing the children the first line of the song, pointing to each button on the score in turn. What do the buttons show? *(The notes of the melody.)*

- Point to the buttons again, repeating for each line of the song. As you do this, the children:

  – hum the melody

  – make the actions

  – hum the melody and make the actions

  Invite a child to play the melody on the prepared xylophone *(pictured above),* using the score as a guide.

- Perform the song with the xylophone accompaniment and with the actions.

Background information

- *Playful pizzicato* is from *Simple Symphony for Strings* by Benjamin Britten (1913-1976).

3 Listen to *Playful pizzicato* to recognise high and low pitch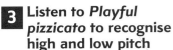

- All listen to tracks 46-48. The music has three sections. Does the middle section sound mostly higher or mostly lower than the beginning and end? *(Lower.)*

- Play the piece again, asking the children to move as they listen, matching their movements to the pitch of the music, eg

  – high: stretch fingertips up and tiptoe

  – low: crouch or slide along

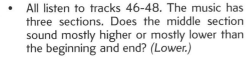

Mary Mac's score

Score 1

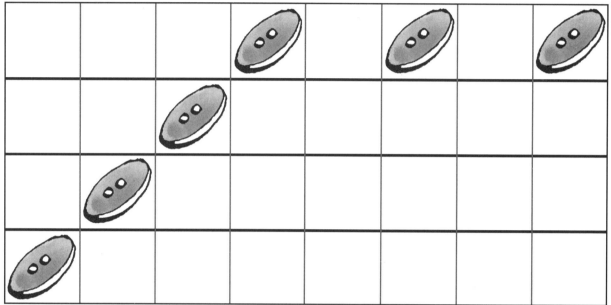

Miss   Ma - ry   Mac   Mac   Mac

Score 2

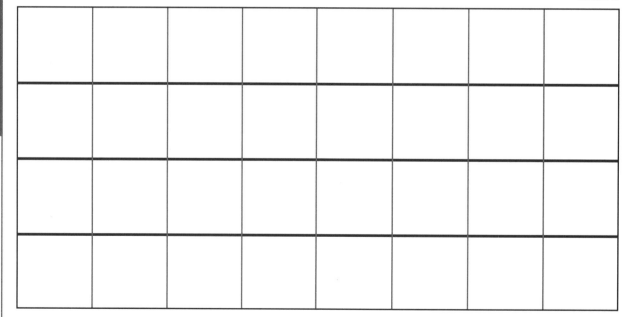

Miss   Ma - ry   Mac   Mac   Mac

MORE HIGH LOW GAMES

1 Listen to *Hot Cross buns* and match the pitch movement to actions and notation

- All listen to the CD. Encourage the children to draw the melody in the air as they listen, just as they did when they listened to *Miss Mary Mac*.

- Sing each line of the song separately and match it with hand movements *(the Hot cross bun cards are here for your reference)*:

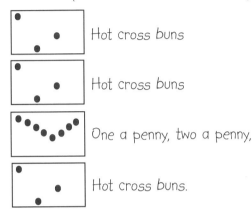

Hot cross buns

Hot cross buns

One a penny, two a penny,

Hot cross buns.

If you have no daughters,

Give them to your sons,

One a penny, two a penny,

Hot cross buns.

Were the hand movements the same for any of the lines? *('Hot cross buns' was performed four times. 'One a penny, two a penny' was performed twice.)*

- Show the children the eight cards from the photocopiable, **Hot cross buns**. Lay them in jumbled order where all can see them.

  All sing the first line of the song. Ask the children to identify the matching card. Repeat, until they have ordered all eight cards.

- Play the CD again. Listen to the song all the way through following the cards. Is the order correct?

3 Compose a new melody for *Miss Mary Mac*

- Revise the song then group the children in pairs. Give each pair a **Mary Mac's score** (Score 2) and a button strip. The children cut the strip into the six buttons. They place the buttons on the grid to show the melody and compare it with Score 1 to check their answer.

- Each pair makes up a new melody by placing the buttons on the card in a new order.

- Invite pairs of children to play their new melody on the prepared xylophone (Lesson 3). The others draw the pitch shape in the air as they sing.

2 Play the tune *Pease pudding hot* using pitch notation

- All listen to the CD. Encourage the children to draw the melody in the air as they listen.

- Sing each line of the song separately and match it with hand movements *(the pitch notation is given for your reference)*:

Pease pudding hot,

Pease pudding cold,

Pease pudding in the pot,

Nine days old.

Were any of the lines the same? *(No.)*

- Show the children the four cards from the photocopiable, **Pease pudding hot**, in jumbled order. Order them as you did in activity 1.

- Invite a child to play the first line on a prepared xylophone. Repeat for the remaining lines.

- Choose a child to select a card and play it. Ask the class to say the matching words.

Hot cross buns

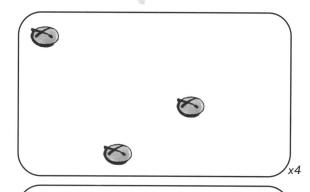

x4

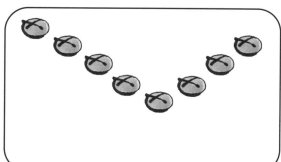

x2

x1

x1

Pease pudding hot

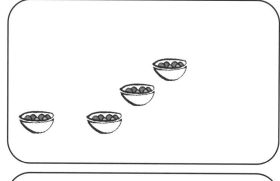

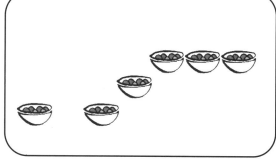

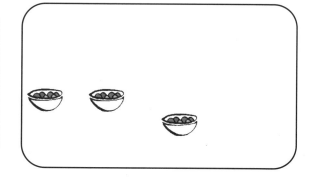

JACK AND THE BEANSTALK

1 **Listen to *Jack and the beanstalk* and respond to pitch movement with vocal sounds**

- The story is told on the CD with sound effects marking the main events. As they listen to the story, the children join in with vocal sound effects, using the full range of their voices from low to high:

  - Beanstalk growing *(swanee whistle)*: slide voices up

  - Jack climbing *(xylophone)*: say 'up up up ...' rising step by step

  - Giant's footsteps *(drum)*: deep 'Boom boom boom boom'

  - Jack climbing down *(xylophone)*: say 'down down down ...' falling step by step

- Encourage the children to move their hands to match the movement of their voices, eg beanstalk growing - slide hand upwards as they slide their voices upwards; Jack climbing - move hands up by step, fist over fist as their voices step up.

2 **Use the *Giant's chant* to explore low voices**

- Practise saying the *Giant's chant* together in low voices:

  Fee fi fo fum
  Watch out kiddies, here I come,
  Run and hide behind your mum,
  Fee fi fo fum.

- From a selection of untuned percussion instruments, find low sounds to accompany the giant chant with a steady beat.

3 **Play the *Giant or Jack?* game to focus listening**

- The class sits in a circle with a selection of untuned percussion instruments and a xylophone in the centre. Place the beanstalk, giant and Jack cards *(opposite)* in a bag. Pass it round the ring as you all say this chant:

  Mighty beanstalk,
  Giant or Jack?
  Who is hiding
  In the sack?

  The child holding the 'sack' at the end of the chant, takes out a card. The child acts as follows:

  - Beanstalk card: child reveals the card and slides it upwards from low to high to signal the others to make a long vocal slide.

  - Giant card: child reveals the card and selects one of the low-pitched instruments to play. The others say the chant and thump the floor with feet or hands, while the child accompanies with the steady beat.

  - Jack card: the child keeps the card hidden and plays the xylophone according to whether Jack is climbing up or climbing down. The others say which it is.

  Having ascertained who is hiding in the sack, all give the response:

  Mighty beanstalk,
  Giant or Jack
  Bean/Giant/Jack was hiding
  In the sack!

Photocopiable cards for Giant or Jack? game

HIGH LOW STORY

1 **Choose instrumental sounds to tell the story of *Jack and the beanstalk***

- Play the CD again all joining in with the vocal sound effects which the children made in lesson 5, activity 1.

- Divide the children into four groups, giving each space to work separately. Give each group their card from the photocopiable, *Jack's story*. Allocate instruments:

  - Group 1: Climbing up the beanstalk step by step

    tuned instruments – glockenspiels, chime bars, xylophones

  - Group 2: Exploring above the clouds

    bells, chime bars, wind chimes (high sounds)

  - Group 3: The giant

    drums, bass xylophone, low keyboards sounds (low sounds)

  - Group 4: Climbing down the beanstalk step by step

    tuned instruments – glockenspiels, chime bars, xylophones

    (Everyone makes vocal sounds for the beanstalk growing.)

- Each group experiments with their instruments and practices playing together. Group 4 practises combining their sounds with saying the *Giant's chant.*

- The groups perform their sounds to the others in order to evaluate whether the pitches match the actions they describe. Make any necessary changes.

2 **Perform the *Jack and the beanstalk* story adding sounds and movement**

- Play the CD pausing at the gaps for the children's music and using the Jack's story cards as a visual reminder of the order:

  - Beanstalk: all

  - Jack climbing: Group 1

  - Exploring: Group 2

  - Giant: Group 3

  - Climbing down: Group 4

Each group plays in turn. All join in with the vocal sounds for the beanstalk growing. All may join in saying the *Giant's chant* while group four plays.

- Record the storytelling and sounds, using a cassette recorder and microphone. Listen to the recording and decide whether any improvements can be made before the final performance.

- Play the recording again and invite the four groups of children to move in response to their music: climbing, exploring, stamping and escaping.

3 **Perform the story to an audience**

- Perform the story to a group of younger children:

  Before the performance begins, each group talks to the audience about the music they will play, displaying their Jack's story card and explaining how the sounds which have been chosen represent the story.

  Three children play the parts of the beanstalk, Jack, and the Giant. These children perform growing, climbing and stamping actions to the groups' music.

Teaching tip

- If you are limited to one CD/cassette player, tell the story yourself so that the performance may be recorded.

- Place the Jack's story cards in the music corner along with a range of instruments so that individuals or pairs may tell the story in sound.

Jack's story

1ˢᵗ

What's the score?
Exploring instruments and symbols

ALL INSTRUMENTAL

Teaching tips
- Encourage the children to join in by miming the action of playing the instruments.
- Track 54 may be used as a backing track if you prefer.

2 Sing *Bang, bang, the sticks go bang* to explore volume

- Listen to the CD together. Ask the children what is different about the first and second halves of each verse. *(First half – loud, second half – quiet.)*

- Divide into four groups, allocating one set of instruments to each:
  - claves (sticks)
  - maracas (shakers)
  - tambours (drums)
  - agogo bells or cowbells (bells)

  Play the first verse on the CD. The sticks group accompany the recording, matching the volume of their playing to the words.

  Bang, bang, the sticks go bang!
  Play as loudly as you can,
  Now as quietly as a mouse,
  Creeping softly round the house.

  Ask the listeners to notice the change in volume from loud to quiet. Did the group accomplish this effectively? Could they improve?

- Repeat, giving each group a turn to play and be assessed:

  Shake shake the shakers shake
  Play the loudest sound they make
  Now as quietly ...

  Boom boom the drums go boom
  Play them loudly in this room ...

  Ting ting the bells go ting
  Play them loudly, make them ring ...

  Ask the listeners to notice ways that individuals play their instruments to produce the different volumes. Are some methods more effective?

- Perform the whole song.

1 Sing *I am the music man* to practise playing instruments

- All listen to the CD to familiarise yourselves with the song.

- The children sit in a circle with a selection of percussion instruments in the centre. A beanbag is passed round while you sing the first part of the song. Whoever is holding the beanbag at 'What can you play?' chooses an instrument and plays while you sing to the end.

  (All sing:)
  I am the music man,
  I come from far away,
  And I can play.
  What can you play? _____
  (Child picks a tambourine and all sing the instrument's name:)

  I play the tambourine.

  (Child plays while all sing:)
  Shake-a shake-a shake-a shake,
  Shake-a shake, shake-a shake,
  Shake-a shake-a shake-a shake,
  Shake-a shake-a shake. *(Repeat.)*

- Play again, inviting a child to select a different instrument, eg
  - drum: tap-a tap-a tap-a tap ...
  - guiro: scrape-a, scrape-a scrape ...

- As it becomes familiar encourage the children to join in singing the song, and to sing the instruments' names themselves.

Teaching tip
- Ensure that the children who are not playing, lay their instruments on the floor or hold them very still.

3 Identify instruments by their sound

- Listen to *Cowboy spring* (track 3) and ask these questions:

  What instrument is making the sound of the horse's feet? *(Coconut shells/woodblock.)*

  Another classroom percussion instrument plays. What is it made of? *(Metal - it is a triangle.)*

- Listen to *Caterpillars only crawl* (track 4) and ask these questions:

  What classroom percussion instrument can you hear at the beginning of the song? *(Tambourine/jingles)*
  Is it playing long or short sounds? *(Long.)*

  In the second part of the music can you hear long or short sounds played on the scraper? *(Long short sequence.)*

LISTEN TO THE BEAT

1 Sing *I can see coconuts* and choose instruments to accompany

- All listen to the CD and join in clapping from 1–10 during the counting sections.
- Ask the children to suggest instruments to make the 'coconut' sounds. Give each child an instrument and sing the song, replacing the claps with instrumental sounds.

I can see coconuts up in the tree.
Coconut water inside them for me.
Let's collect coconuts, one, two, three, four,
Shake the tree, shake the tree,
I'd like some more.

One, two, three, four, five, six, seven, eight, nine, ten.

One, two, three, four, five, six, seven, eight, nine, ten.

3 Listen to *Rainforest music* to identify volume

- Listen to the CD together. What sounds can the children identify in the music?

  - monkeys, birds, insects, frogs, rain, thunder

- Listen again, asking the children to focus on the volume of sound they hear. Can they describe how the volume changes?

  - monkeys, birds, insects and frogs *(loud then getting quieter)*;

  - silence;

  - rain dripping and pattering on leaves *(very quiet)*;

  - thunder rolling far off, approaching and going away *(getting louder, then quieter)*;

  - monkeys, birds, insects and frogs *(loud)*.

2 Listen to *Slowly slowly* and explore playing slowly and quickly

- As they listen to the CD the children use hand and finger actions to describe the words they hear:

Slowly, slowly, very slowly
Creeps the garden snail.
Slowly, slowly, very slowly
Up the wooden rail.

Quickly, quickly, very quickly
Runs the little mouse.
Quickly, quickly, very quickly
Round about the house.

- Give everyone a small hand held percussion instrument. As they listen again, they accompany the words by playing slowly then quickly. Encourage the children to play on the beat once they have explored playing freely:

Slow - ly, slow - ly ...

Quick - ly, quick - ly, ve - ry quick - ly ...

- Sing the song without the CD, singing and playing the slow section even slower, the fast section even faster.

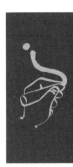

3rd

What's the score?
Exploring instruments and symbols

SOUND SHAPES

1 Use the *Coconuts* score to match notation with sound

- Sing *I can see coconuts* together. As you sing, show the children *Coconuts score* (score 1), and point to each black coconut in turn as the children clap and sing the ten counts twice at the end of the song.

- Turn the score over and ask if they can suggest what to do when they see the empty coconut symbols. (*They count but do not clap the beats.*)

Practise singing the counting section while shaking both hands in the air on each beat to mark it silently.

- Invite a child to conduct by choosing which side of the card to display to the others. The children respond by clapping each beat or marking them silently. Confident conductors can change the card round at the end of the first count of ten.

2 Sing *When you play the tambour* to explore graphic symbols

- All listen to the CD:

When you play the tambour,
What sound will you make?
Using hand or beater,
Tap or slide or scrape.

Ask the children to tell you the sequence of the sounds they heard after the song. (*Scrape, tap, slide.*)

- Ask a volunteer to demonstrate a tap, slide and scrape on a tambour using fingers, hands or a beater.

- The children sit in a circle. A tambour is passed round while you sing the song. The child holding the tambour at the end chooses a way to play a new sequence of three sounds, eg tap, scrape, slide.

- Show the class the three symbols from the *Tap slide scrape* photocopiable. Discuss with the class which of these might best represent the tambour sounds:

    (tap)

─────   (slide)

wwww   (scrape)

- Sing the song again. This time the player orders the symbols first, then plays the corresponding sequence.

- Play the game again using a different instrument, eg a cowbell. How many ways can the children find to play this? Discuss how the sounds might be written graphically. Will a tapping sound on a cowbell look the same or different from a tapping sound on a tambour? Use the blank spaces to notate ideas. (*You may need more or fewer than three for each instrument.*)

3 Sing *Jenny, tap the sticks* to revise playing instruments loudly and quietly

- Listen to the CD to familiarise yourselves with the song.

(Jenny), tap the sticks,
Tap them very loudly,
(Jenny), tap the sticks,
Tap them very loudly.

(Jenny), tap the sticks,
Tap them very quietly,
(Jenny), tap the sticks,
Tap them very quietly.

- The children sit in a circle with a selection of instruments in the centre. Invite one child to choose an instrument and play while everyone else sings. Play and sing loudly then quietly as directed by the words.

- Change to a new player, and a new instrument, eg

(Samir), shake the bells,
Shake them very loudly ...

Coconuts score

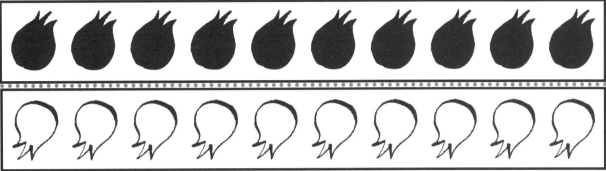

Enlarge onto card, and fold along the dotted line   Score 1

Extension: blank copy to enlarge and fill in   Score 2

Tap slide scrape

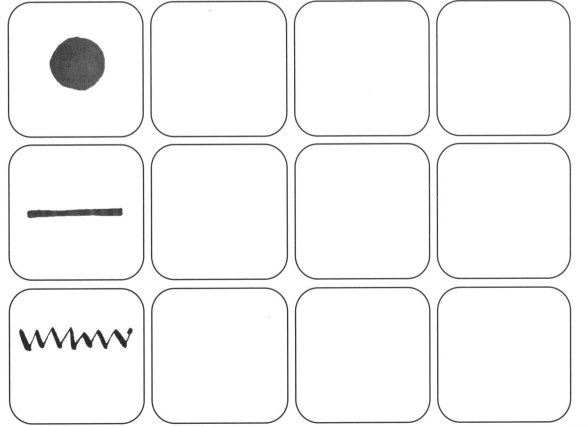

BE LOUD! BE QUIET!

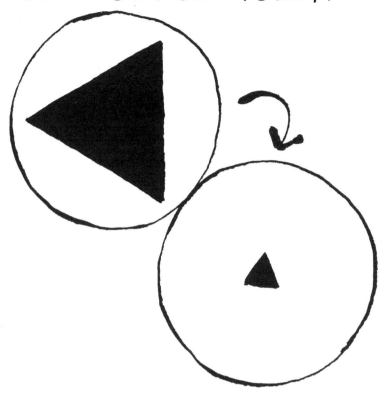

1 **Sing *Jenny, tap the sticks* responding to symbols**

- Sing the song together. One of the children taps claves, loudly then quietly as in Lesson 3.

- Decide together on a symbol to use for the sound of tapping claves ('sticks'), eg

- On a large circle of paper (about 30 cm in diameter) draw a very large version of the symbol and on the reverse of the circle draw a very small version.

  Ask the children what they think the large version means? *(Play loudly.)* Ask what the small version means. *(Play quietly.)*

- Invite a child to conduct by placing the circle on the floor in front of the claves player. Ask the children how the player should play - loudly or quietly? Everyone then sings the song accordingly, while the player plays.

  The conductor may turn the card over at any point in the song - all respond accordingly, eg *(reference track 10a)*:

  Jenny, tap the sticks,
  Tap them very quietly ..
  Jenny, tap the sticks,
  Tap them very loudly.

- Select a new instrument and decide on a new symbol. Draw it again on another circle of paper. Sing again with a different player and conductor *(reference track 10b)*:

  Samir shake the bells ...

2 **Sing and play *Silence and sound* responding to graphic symbols for volume**

- Listen to CD track 11 to familiarise yourselves with the song.

- The children sit in a circle each with a small hand-held instrument placed ready to play.

  Show the children the *Silence and sound* cards. What does each graphic symbol indicate?

- Pass the *Composer* and *Conductor* cards round as you sing the song. The two children holding the cards at the end are appointed to these roles.

  Use the cards, change them round,
  Some show silence, some show sound,
  So our music changes in a clever way.
  Who will show us what to play?

- The composer selects and arranges four of the cards from left to right. The conductor slowly moves a pointer along the cards and everyone plays freely and continuously at the appropriate volume or keeps silent. *(Reference track 12.)*

- Was the composer pleased with the result? Did the players respond well to the symbols?

3 **Listen to *Rainforest music* and match volume to symbols and movement**

- All listen to *Rainforest music* and notice again how the volume changes (Lesson 2, activity 3).

  Can the children order the *Silence and sound* cards to match the music? All listen again to check the order.

- Listen again, inviting the children to make movements which match in size the volume as it changes.

Silence and sound

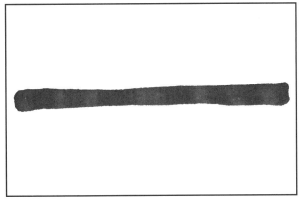

play very quietly

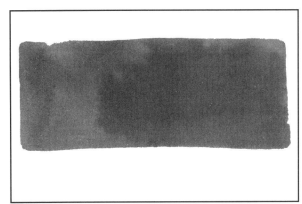

play very loudly

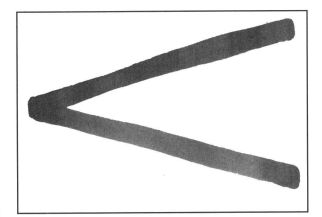

get louder

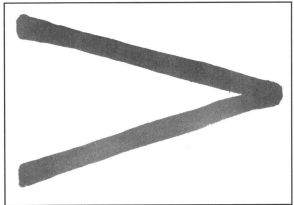

get quieter

Composer

Conductor

silence

Music Express Year 1 © A & C Black 2002
www.acblack.com/musicexpress

What's the score?
Exploring instruments and symbols

TREASURE ISLAND TRAILER

1 Sing Yo ho ho and make footstep sounds

- Listen to the CD. All join in singing the song as it becomes familiar:

  Yo ho ho, me mates,
  A pirate's life for me,
  Off to find a treasure chest
  On an island in the sea.

- Encourage the children to rock from side to side to the beat of the music as they sing:

- Sing again, this time adding footstep sounds after the song by tapping alternate fists on knees to the steady rocking beat.

- Show the children the footstep cards. Place eight of the cards in a row along the floor. Ask the children to count them. Practise together, tapping fists on knees for each of the counts. Sing the song again, rocking from side to side. At the end, tap fists on knees for each of the eight footsteps.

- Invite a child to change the number of footsteps. All sing again. Check that all the children are responding accurately to the number of footsteps.

3 Notate music for the island scenes

- Look at *Island scenes 2* together. Discuss the sounds the class might choose to describe each scene using vocal, body and instrumental sounds.

- Divide the class into three groups – one for each scene. Give each group a copy of their scene and invite each in turn to choose instruments for their work from a large selection.

  Allow the groups time and space in which to experiment with their island scene sounds. Each group may need to appoint a conductor to direct them using a traffic light signal (page 12).

- The groups take turns to play their music to the others.

  As a class, suggest ways of drawing or writing the sounds for each group's music on the space below the scene. Talk about the choices the children have for doing this based on the previous activity.

- Complete a notation for each group using the ideas from the whole class.

2 Discuss sound and notation for each of the island scenes p51

- Explain the story briefly: that three pirates find Captain Bone's treasure map and sail away to his island to find the hidden gold.

  Show the children *Island scenes 1*. What sounds do the pictures suggest?

  (Noisy monkeys and falling coconuts, bubbly water and darting fish, thunder storm approaching and going away.)

- Look at the way these sounds are notated below each scene:

  – monkey vocal sounds and a coconut strip showing sound and silence

  – a water bottle and straw for continuous bubbly sounds and for darting fish

  – graphic symbols indicating an increase then a decrease of volume with loud crashes in the middle.

- Talk about the many ways in which sounds may be notated. Remind the children of some of the scores they have used in other units as well as this one:

  – coconut strips indicating a pattern of sounds, p47

  – symbols for instrumental sounds, p47

  – loud and quiet indicated by size; getting louder and getting quieter signs, p49

  – fireworks pictures, p17

  – dragon picture showing selected instruments, p33

  – City sounds trail, p15

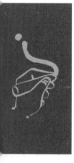

Island scenes 1

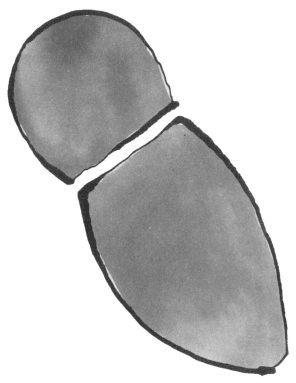

5th

What's the score?
Exploring instruments and symbols

Photocopiable

Island scenes 2

TREASURE ISLAND PERFORMANCE

1 **Play a game to complete a score of *Treasure Island* music**

- Arrange the three island groups round an enlarged copy of the Treasure Island map (CD-ROM). Beside it place face down the class notations of the island scenes from Lesson 5 activity 3.

  The footsteps on the map show how far the pirates walk between each scene and which direction they take; tap fists on knees after singing the song each time and according to the number of steps.

- Play the game like this. You control the CD player or tell the story yourself. At the words 'This is what they saw' pause the CD and choose a child to turn over one of the island scenes and place it in the first blank space on the map. The corresponding group plays their music. When the music finishes, the story resumes until the map score is complete, and all three groups have played their music.

Teaching tip

To familiarise the children with the story and to practise score reading, read the story without the music while following the pirates' path on the Treasure Island score.

2 **Rehearse a performance of *Treasure Island***

- Give the groups time and space to refine their island scenes, then join together to rehearse a complete performance following the *Treasure Island* score:
  - you or a child tell the story
  - all sing and rock for *Yo ho ho*, then tap knees for each footstep on the map
  - each group plays their island scene in turn
  - all join in with Captain Bone's voice.

3 **Perform and record *Treasure Island***

- Perform *Treasure Island* as rehearsed above. Record the performance on a cassette player.
- Play back the recording. The children listen as they follow the score.
- Give the recording to another class to enjoy the story.

Once there were three pirates who found Captain Bone's old treasure map and went looking for his gold. They rowed to the treasure island, studied the map and set off down the path leading to the treasure chest.

> Yo ho ho ... (FOOTSTEPS)
> And this is what they saw - (MUSIC)
>
> Off they went along the track again.
> Yo ho ho ... (FOOTSTEPS)
> And this is what they saw (MUSIC)
>
> Off they went along the track again.
> Yo ho ho ... (FOOTSTEPS)
> And this is what they saw (MUSIC)
>
> Off they went along the track again.
> Yo ho ho ... (FOOTSTEPS)

And there they were at last, at the end of the trail, with a *beautiful big treasure chest* right in front of their greedy noses. They all grabbed the lid and opened it. But this is what they heard -

> This is the voice of Captain Bone
> Leave my treasure chest ALONE!

'Help!' shouted the pirates — and they dropped the map and ran for their lives.

> (FOOTSTEPS - fast)

Off they rowed back to the safety of their ship — never to be seen again. And, back on the island, Benjamin Bone's old parrot chuckled to itself before tucking its head under its wing and settling down to sleep on the Captain's treasure chest.

MINIBEAST MANOEUVRES

1 **Listen to *Playful pizzicato* to describe minibeasts in movement**

- Explain to the children that the first section of the music they will hear could describe a garden busy with minibeasts. Play the CD *(track 15)*. What minibeasts do they imagine as they listen to the music? *(eg bees, ants, butterflies, crickets, beetles).*

- Listen again to track 15. The children individually choose a minibeast and move lightly and quickly as the music plays.

- Listen to the second section of the music *(track 16)*. Tell the children that a gardener has arrived to do some work. As they listen, the children act out the jobs the gardener might be doing *(eg, digging, raking, cutting, mowing, pushing a wheelbarrow).*

- What is the difference between the minibeast movements and the gardener's movements? *(The first are light and quick, the second are heavy, strong and slow.)*

- Play the last section *(track 17)*. The children will hear minibeast music and the gardener again, and respond appropriately in movement.

- Move to the complete piece of music *(tracks 15-17).*

Background information

- Playful pizzicato is from Simple Symphony for Strings by Benjamin Britten (1913-1976).

2 **Sing the action song *Says the bee***

- All listen to the CD, joining in singing as it becomes familiar.

  Come with me, says the bee,
  Into the daffodil.
  All our house has yellow walls,
  And honey on the sill.

  Come with me, says the bee,
  Into the open rose.
  Perfume curtains all around,
  And pollen on your toes.

  Come with me, says the bee,
  Into the lily flower.
  Sun in your window every sunny day,
  Umbrella for a shower.

Encourage the children to sing expressively using short light sounds to suggest the movements of the bee.

- Add fingerplay actions.

- When the song is familiar, choose a small group of children to accompany by vocally buzzing the melody.

3 **Listen to *Lots of worms* and respond with movement**

- As they listen to the CD, ask the children to find movements with hands and arms to give the idea of worms moving underground.

- How are the sounds in the song different from the sounds in *Says the bee?* *(Longer, slower, lower, smoother.)*

MINIBEAST BAND

1 Choose sounds to accompany *Says the bee*

- Show the children a kazoo and buzz the melody of *Says the bee* to demonstrate the kazoo. Show them how to obtain a kazoo sound with a paper and comb. Invite a small group of children to buzz comb kazoos as the rest of the class sing.

- From a selection of small classroom percussion, eg egg maracas, small drums, claves, wind chimes, encourage the children to choose sounds to accompany the end of each verse - honey, pollen, shower.

2 Sing *Lots of worms* and add an instrumental accompaniment

- All listen to the CD, joining in singing as it becomes familiar.

> Well, there are lots of worms
>   way under the ground,
> Lots of worms that I've never found,
> I'll bet they're way down there
>   a-diggin' around
> Way under the ground.

Encourage the children to sing the song expressively, using long sounds, deep voices, and a slow speed.

- From a selection of small classroom percussion instruments, ask the children to choose sounds which describe the worm, eg long scraping sounds on a drum skin, crackling sounds on a piece of cellophane, a scraper, hand chime (note A).

- Add a drone. Play a steady beat on a xylophone or metallophone throughout:

```
          A       A       A
Well there are lots  of  worms way under  ...
```

- Perform the song with the chosen accompaniments.

3 Listen to *Bird calls* and improvise vocal patterns

- What does the music describe? (*Birds calls.*)

- How many birds are singing together? (*Two.*)

- Listen again, joining in with the bird which has the same song throughout (*oo–oooooo, oo–oooooo, oo–oooooo*).

- Play this pattern on a chime bar, note F, and ask the children to join in with their voices singing 'oo ooooo'.

- Collect from the class descriptive words for familiar bird calls (*eg tweet, chitter chitter, crooo crooo, cuckoo, twit twooo, peeep*).

- Divide the class into two groups. The first group join in with the chime bar pattern, which may be played by a confident child. The second group add their bird calls freely.

GARDENS IN THE RAIN

1 **Sing *Rillaby rill* and add an instrumental accompaniment**

- All listen to the CD, joining in singing as it becomes familiar:

  Grasshoppers three a-fiddling went,
  Hey ho never be still,
  They paid no money toward the rent,
  But all day long with their elbows bent,
  They fiddled a tune called rillaby rillaby
  Fiddled a tune called rillaby rill.

- From a selection of small classroom percussion instruments and soundmakers, ask the children to choose sounds which describe the grasshopper, eg a comb scraped with a pencil tip, corrugated card scraped with fingernails, finger-rings made of sandpaper scraped together.

- Accompany the song with the chosen sounds playing a steady beat throughout the song, to the words:

| Hey | ho | Hey | ho | Hey | ho |

2 **Listen to and discuss *Gardens in the rain***

- How does the music describe a garden in the rain?

  (Rippling, dripping sounds, high and low sounds, fast sounds which get louder and quieter.)

> ### Background information
>
> ***Gardens in the rain*** is by the French composer Debussy who wrote during the Impressionist period in art and music and wrote many highly descriptive pieces of piano music.

3 **Sing *Rain rain go away* and add body percussion, responding to a graphic score** p57

- Listen to the CD and join in singing as it becomes familiar:

  Rain rain go away,
  Come again another day.

- Find ways of making rain sounds using tongue clicks, finger taps, hand claps, knee and chest taps. As a class, order the sounds from quietest to loudest.

- Conduct a rainstorm with your hands - start with palms together, gradually move them apart, then back together again. *(When your palms are together the children are silent, at their widest they make their loudest sounds.)* Sit very still in silence at the end.

- Now use the Rain score. Show the children the score and discuss how it represents the sounds getting louder and quieter. Perform the rain sounds again, this time moving a pointer across the score from left to right, observing the silence at the end.

- Perform *Rain rain go away* in this order:

A: song   B: rain sounds   C: silence

Rain rain
go away,
Come again
another day.

Rain score

cut out and join together into one long score, see p56

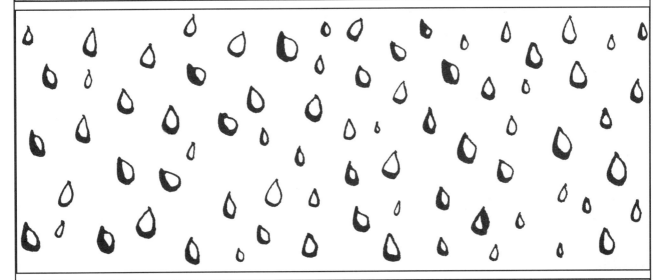

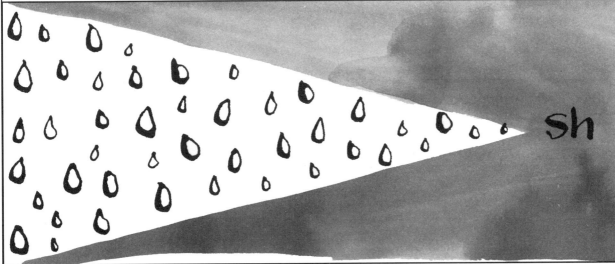

WHEN THE RAIN STOPS

1 Listen to *Shall I sing?* and add movement

- Add actions in lines two and four:

Shall I bloom says the flower?
(fingers open like a flower)

Shall I fall says the shower?
(fingers wiggle like rain falling)

- Show the children the *April showers* score. Discuss the movements the children might make for lark, sun, grasshopper and ant. Remind them of the movements they found for bee and worm.

- Listen to the song again. As you point to each of the six pictures in turn, the children respond with matching actions.

Teaching tips

- Ensure that the children understand how to treat the instruments with care when playing loudly. Instruments should never be struck forcibly. Demonstrate how to play loudly without using force.

- Avoid using the word 'hit'. Instead encourage the children to use the words 'play', 'strike' or 'tap'.

2 Choose instrumental sounds to accompany *Rain rain go away*

- Remind the children of the body percussion they made for rain. Give everyone an instrument, eg castanets, maracas, woodblocks, hand drums, claves, indian bells.

Discuss how the sounds can increase in volume this time. *(Each player needs to increase the volume of their playing.)*

- Choose one child to conduct, using the hand signal from before. Perform the rain sounds on the instruments.

Did the rain start gently and quietly, gradually grow louder, and fade away to silence at the end? How can the performance be improved?

- Perform *Rain rain go away* in this order:

Section A: song   Section B: rain sounds - silence

Rain rain go away, Come again another day.

3 Draw the sounds onto the *April showers* score

- Using a wide range of instruments and sound makers, discuss and try out with the children the sounds they might choose for each picture, reminding them of those they have already found and finding new sounds for the others.

- Give pairs of children a photocopy each of a verse from the score, allocating the three verses evenly round the class. Each pair finds a way to draw their chosen sounds onto the blank spaces in the score. They may choose to draw the instruments they have chosen, the word patterns, or a graphic of the sound.

- Invite pairs of children to play the sounds for their verse. How well do their sounds describe the pictures? Have they chosen a good way to represent the sounds?

April showers score

Rain rain
go away,
Come again
another day.

sh

Rain rain
go away,
Come again
another day.

sh

Rain rain
go away,
Come again
another day.

sh

5th Rain rain go away
Exploring timbre, tempo and dynamics

SUN AND RAIN REHEARSALS

1 Learn *Shall I sing?* p59 24)))

* Listen to the CD to familiarise yourselves with the song.

> Shall I sing? *says the lark,*
> Shall I bloom? *says the flower,*
> Shall I come? *says the sun,*
> Shall I fall? *says the shower.*
>
> Shall I buzz? *says the bee,*
> Shall I bloom? *says the flower,*
> Shall I wiggle? *says the worm,*
> Shall I fall? *says the shower.*
>
> Shall I hop? *says grasshopper,*
> Shall I bloom? *says the flower,*
> Shall I march? *says the ant,*
> Shall I fall? *says the shower.*

> **Teaching tips**
> Use the score to remind the children of the order of the words.

2 Practise playing the *Shall I sing?* interludes 24)))

* Divide the children into pairs as before, grouping the pairs together - one group per verse.

  Each child in each pair selects one of the two pictures, chooses their instrumental sound and practises playing in turn.

* All sing verse one, making the actions for lines two and four. At the end of line one the larks in each group play their sounds. At the end of line three, the suns play.

* Repeat for each verse.

3 Add sounds to the recording of *Rain rain go away* p59 25)))

* Listen to the CD. The children join in with the *Rain rain go away* song and during the instrumental section following, they add their own instrumental sounds. You will need to discuss how best to time getting louder and getting quieter so that it fits the backing track and ends with silence. Practise this. *(You may need to conduct this yourself using the hand signals from before.)*

* As a class, decide on a way to draw the rain getting louder then quieter on the rain sections of the *April showers* score.

APRIL SHOWERS

1 **Prepare a complete score for**
April showers, a class composition

- As a class, collect the scoring ideas from each *Shall I sing?* verse
group, and from everyone for the *Rain rain go away* section, and
record these on the blank class score (an enlarged version of *April*
showers, p59).

  Arrange the sections of the score from left to right where everyone
can see them *(see below)*.

- Divide into three groups as before. Practise each of the sounds in
order, according to the score and using backing track 26. All children
play the rain sections on body percussion.

   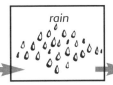 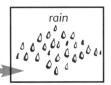

2 **Prepare the performance of**
April showers

- Sing the song with the actions. Everyone uses body percussion for
the rain sections. Follow the class score to reinforce the structure.

- Divide into the three groups. Sing the song adding the instrumental
sounds for each verse *(individual groups)* and the instrumental
sounds for the rain sections *(everyone, using their instruments)*.

- Record your rehearsal. Play back the recording and discuss ways of
improving the performance. Was there a silence at the end of each
rain section? How well did everyone control volume? How
expressively did the children use their voices during the verses? Can
they make a contrast between their singing of the verses *(quiet and*
light) and their singing of the rain song *(louder and stronger)*.

3 **Perform April showers**

- Perform *April showers* in an assembly about life in a garden.

  Incorporate the other songs and music from this unit:

  – *Says the bee*

  – *There are lots of worms*

  – *Bird calls*

  – *Rillaby rill*

  – *Gardens in the rain*

  – *Playful pizzicato*

Index

Index of songs, stories and chants (titles and *first lines*)

Videoclips

Audio CD 1-2 track list

Track Contents CD 1

Sounds interesting

1a/b   *Sound song* (page 8)
2   *Hands can hold* (8)
3   *Sounds menu* (10)
4   *Choose an instrument* (11)
5   *Listen to the east* (11)
6   *Play it to the east* (11)
7   *The big blue jeep and the little white trike* (12, 13)
8   *The wheels on the bus* (13)
9   *The little train of the Caipira* (14)
10   *Sing a song of people* (14)
11   *Sing a song of people* - backing track (14)

The long and the short of it

12   *Some sounds are short* (16)
13   *Firework sounds* (16)
14   *Fireworks bingo* (16)
15   *It's bonfire night* (18)
16   *Fade or float?* (19)
17   *Rippling rhythm* (20)
18   *Ho! Jack Frost* (20, 21)
19   *Coming down* (21, 22)
20   *Coming down* - backing track (22)

Feel the pulse

21   *Pinocchio* (24)
22   *Pinocchio* - hand clapping (24)
23   *Raga abhogi* (24)
24   *Country dance* (24)
25   *Okki-tokki-unga* (24)
26a   *Get on board* (25)
26b   *Get on board* - changing speed (25)
27   *Bransle de chevaux* (25)
28   *I hear thunder* - clapping the beat (26)
29   *Thunder rhythms* (26)
30   *I hear thunder* - clapping the rhythm(26)
31a   *Okki-tokki-unga* - chorus (26)
31b   - chorus word rhythms (26)
31c   - combined beat and rhythm (26)
32   *This old man* - clapping the beat (28)
33   *This old man* - word rhythms (28)
34   *This old man* - rhythms line by line (28)
35   *This old man* - sample rhythm pattern (28)
36   *This old man* - drum ostinato (28)
37   *Clap your hands* (28)
38   *This old man* - sample improvisation (30)
39   *Clap and wiggle* - sample rhythm pattern (30)

Track Contents CD 1/2

40   *A dragon's very fierce* (30, 32)
41a   Dragon drone accompaniment (32)
41b   Dragon ostinato accompaniment (32)
41c   *A dragon's very fierce* - performance (32)

Taking off

42   *Five little froggies* (34)
43   *Slide song* (36)
44   *Jack's game* (36)
45   *Miss Mary Mac* (36, 37)
46   *Playful pizzicato* - section 1(37, 54)
47   *Playful pizzicato* - section 2(37, 54)
48   *Playful pizzicato* - section 3(37, 54)
49   *Hot cross buns* (39)
50   *Pease pudding hot* (39)
51   *Jack and the beanstalk* (41, 42)
52   *Giant's chant* (41)
53   *Jack and the beanstalk* - with gaps (42)

What's the score? CD 2

1   *I am the music man* (44)
2   *Bang, bang the sticks go bang* (44)
3   *Cowboy spring*   (44)
4   *Caterpillars only crawl* (44)
5   *I can see coconuts* (45)
6   *Slowly slowly* (45)
7   *Rainforest music* (45, 48)
8   *When you play the tambour* (46)
9   *Jenny, tap the sticks* (46)
10a   *Jenny, tap the sticks* - first sample (48)
10b   *Jenny, tap the sticks* - second sample (48)
11   *Silence and sound* (48)
12   *Silence and sound* - sample composition (48)
13   *Yo ho ho* (50)
14   *Treasure island* (53)

Rain rain go away

15   *Playful pizzicato* - section 1(37, 54)
16   *Playful pizzicato* - section 2(37, 54)
17   *Playful pizzicato* - section 3(37, 54)
18   *Says the bee* (54, 55)
19   *Lots of worms* (54, 55)
20   *Bird calls* (55)
21   *Rillaby rill* (56)
22   *Gardens in the rain* (56)
23   *Rain rain go away* - chant (56)
24   *Shall I sing?* (58, 60)
25   *Rain rain go away* - backing track (60)
26   *April showers* - backing track (61)

Acknowledgements

The author and publishers would like to thank all the teachers and consultants who assisted in the preparation of this series: Meriel Ascott, Francesca Bedford, Chris Bryant, Yolanda Cattle, Stephen Chadwick, Veronica Clark, Tania Demidova, Adrian Downie, Veronica Hanke, Maureen Hanke, Emily Haward, Jocelyn Lucas, Carla Moss, Danny Monte, Lio Moscardini, Sue Nicholls, Vanessa Olney, Mrs S. Pennington, Pauline Quinton, Ana Sanderson, Jane Sebba, Heather Scott, Michelle Simpson, Debbie Townsend and Joy Woodall.

Winston Lewis, Debbie Sanders, Missak Takoushian and Vivien Ellis performed the songs and chants recorded for the CD. Thanks are also due to all who performed for previous recordings for A&C Black publications which have been reused in *Music Express Year 1*. Helen MacGregor, the staff and children of Grafton Infant School, and the Year 1 and 3 children of Brunswick Park Primary School performed the activities demonstrated on the CD-ROM videoclips.

The following copyright material has been created for *Music Express* by A&C Black or is previously published in A&C Black publications:

A dragon's very fierce, Bang, bang the sticks go bang, Choose an instrument, Clap your hands and wiggle your fingers, Some sounds are short, words by Sue Nicholls from *Bobby Shaftoe, clap your hands*, published by A&C Black, © 1992.

The big blue jeep and little white trike, Pinocchio from *Three Tapping Teddies* by Kaye Umansky, published by A&C Black, © 2000

Fade or float, Jenny tap the sticks (*Jenny play the drum*), *Silence and Sound, When you play the tambour*, words by Sue Nicholls from *Michael Finnigin, tap your chinigin*, published by A&C Black, © 1998.

Get on board by Helen MacGregor from *Listening to Music 5+*, published by A&C Black © 1995.

Hands can hold and hands can squeeze, words by Veronica Clark to traditional melody, from *High Low Dolly Pepper*, published by A&C Black, © 1991.

Jack and the beanstalk, Treasure Island, Yo ho ho, me mates by Kaye Umansky, and *Jack's song* by Helen MacGregor from *Three Singing Pigs*, published by A&C Black, © 1994.

Shall I sing? (April) words adapted from traditional by Helen MacGregor and Sheena Roberts, music by Neville Favell, from *Harlequin* published by A&C Black.

Sounds menu and *Rainforest music* by Stephen Chadwick created for *Music Express*, © 2002

I hear thunder and *Hot cross buns* from *Sing Hey Diddle Diddle*; *I am the music man, Miss Mary Mac, Okki-tokki-unga* and *This old man* from *Okki-tokki-unga*; *Pease pudding hot* from *Flying a Round*; *Rillaby rill* from *Birds and Beasts*; *Rain rain go away*; traditional words and melody, arranged and recorded by A&C Black.

The following copyright holders have kindly given their permission for the inclusion of their copyright material in the book and on the audio CD:

Bird calls from EUCD 1553 *Bushmen – Quii – First people*. By permission of ARC Music Productions International Ltd.

Bransle de chevaux, performed by Piffaro. Licensed by kind permission from the Film & TV Licensing division, part of the Universal Music Group, courtesy of Deutsche Grammophon.

Bubble from *Playsongs* by Sheena Roberts, © 1987.

Caterpillars only crawl by Peter Charlton and Sue Charlton © 1972 Keith Prowse Music Publishing Co Ltd (MCPS).

Coming down by Jill Darby © 1980 BTW Music.

Country dance from Suite no 3 in G (The Water Music) by Handel.

Performed by the Bath Festival Orchestra, conducted by Yehudi Menuhin. Recording © 1964. Classics for Pleasure cat no CD CFP 4698. Digital remastering ℗ 1989 by EMI Records Ltd.

Cowboy spring from the *Children's Song Book* by Elizabeth Poston, published by The Bodley Head. Used by permission of The Random House Group Ltd (MCPS).

Five little froggies, adapted from traditional by Helen MacGregor, from *Five little frogs* arranged, produced and recorded by Playsongs Publications, © 1998.

Gardens in the rain (*Jardins sous la pluie* from *Estampes*) by Debussy: performed by Jean-Bernard Pommier (piano) ℗ 1989. The copyright in this sound recording is owned by EMI Records Ltd. Virgin Classics. Licensed courtesy of EMI Commercial Markets.

Ho! Jack Frost. Words by Helen Call. Music by Mary Root Kern. © 1941 (renewed) Summy-Birchard Music, a division of Summy Birchard Inc, USA. Warner/Chappell Music Ltd London W6 8BS. Reproduced by permission of International Music Publications Ltd. All Rights Reserved.

I can see coconuts adapted with new words by Helen MacGregor from *I can see cherries* by Wendy van Blankenstein.

It's bonfire night by Leslie Lees from *Jump in the Ring*. By permission of Ward Lock Educational Company Limited. (MCPS.)

Listen to the east, words and melody by Sheena Roberts, © 1995. (MCPS.)

The little train of the Caipira by Heitor Villa-Lobos, performed by the London Symphony Orchestra, conducted by Sir Eugene Goossens. An Everest recording, courtesy of the Omega Record Group Inc. (MCPS.)

Lots of worms, words and music by Patty Zeitlin, © Bullfrog Ballades, used by permission of Folkllore Productions Inc.

Playful pizzicato from *Simple Symphony* Opus 4: 2 by Benjamin Britten. Performed by Orpheus Chamber Orchestra. Courtesy of Deutsch Grammophon. Licensed by kind permission from the Film & TV Licensing division, part of the Universal Music Group. (MCPS.)

Raga abhogi, from the *Raga Guide* CD NI 5536 Wyastone Estate Limited trading as Nimbus Records, www.wyastone.co.uk.

Rippling rhythm. Shapiro Bernstein & Co for *Rippling rhythm* (Gioe Fields) © by Shapiro Bernstein & Co Ltd, London W1V 5TZ.

Says the bee, words and music by Malvina Reynolds. Copyright 1961 by Schroder Music Co (ASCAP). Renewed 1989. Used by permission. All rights reserved.

Sing a song of people words copyright Lois Lenski 1956, music by Chris Cameron, published in *Tinderbox* by A&C Black, © 1982.

The slide song words and music by Sue Nicholls © 1992.

Slowly slowly, words traditional, melody (*Slowly walks my grandad*) by A W I Chitty, Paxton Music Ltd, arranged and recorded for Sleepy Time Playsongs by Playsongs Publications. All rights reserved. (MCPS.)

Sound song, words and music by Harriet Powell from *Game-songs with Prof Dogg's Troupe* created by Ed Berman, published by A & C Black Publishers Ltd. Used by permission.

The wheels on the bus arranged and recorded for *Sleepy Time Playsongs* by Playsongs Publications, © 1995. (MCPS.)

Music Express Year 1 CD and CD-ROM © and ℗ 2002 A&C Black Publishers Ltd. All rights of the owner of the works reproduced reserved. Unauthorised copying, hiring, lending, public performace and broadcasting of these recordings and videoclips prohibited.

Every effort has been made to trace and acknowledge copyright owners. If any right has been omitted, the publishers offer their apologies and will rectify this in subsequent editions following notification.